El
of
no

D1333877

GREECE AND ROME LIVE

Also available in this series:

Forthcoming titles:

ANCIENT ROME
AT THE CINEMA

STORY AND SPECTACLE IN
HOLLYWOOD AND ROME

Elena Theodorakopoulos

BRISTOL
PHOENIX
PRESS

For Tessa and Nikos

Paperback cover image: *Pollice Verso* ('Thumbs Down'), 1872 (oil on canvas) by
Jean Leon Gerome (1824–1904) (courtesy of Phoenix Art Museum, Arizona,
USA/Bridgeman Art Library)

First published in 2010 by
Bristol Phoenix Press
an imprint of The Exeter Press
Reed Hall, Streatham Drive
Exeter EX4 4QR
UK
www.exeterpress.co.uk

British Library Cataloguing in Publication Data
A catalogue record for this book is available
from the British Library.

Hardback ISBN 978 1 904675 54 9
Paperback ISBN 978 1 904675 28 0

Typeset in Chaparral Pro 11.5pt on 15pt
by JCS Publishing Services Ltd, www.jcs-publishing.co.uk

Printed in Great Britain by Short Run Press Ltd

Mixed Sources
Product group from well-managed
forests and other controlled sources
www.fsc.org Cert no. SA-COC-002112
© 1996 Forest Stewardship Council

FSC

CONTENTS

ILLUSTRATIONS

To have all those noble Romans alive before me, and walking in and out for my entertainment, instead of being the stern taskmasters they had been at school, was a most novel and delightful effect. But the mingled reality and mystery of the whole show, the influence upon me of the poetry, the lights, the music, the company, the smooth stupendous changes of glittering and brilliant scenery, were so dazzling, and opened up such illimitable regions of delight, that when I came out into the rainy street, at twelve o'clock at night, I felt as if I had come from the clouds, where I had been leading a romantic life for ages, to a bawling, splashing, link-lighted, umbrella-struggling, hackney-coach-jostling, patten-clinking, muddy, miserable world.

(Charles Dickens, *David Copperfield*)

INTRODUCTION

This book is about how films invent the world of ancient Rome, and about the stories they tell. I have selected four examples of mainstream historical drama beginning with *Ben-Hur* (1959) and ending with *Gladiator* (2000) and two examples of independent films, *Fellini Satyricon* (1969) and *Titus* (1999). The historical epics of the 1950s and 1960s that I have chosen formed a big part of Hollywood's attempt to lure audiences away from the television screen and into the movie theatre. To achieve this, they were often dominated by extravagant displays of spectacle, including for instance the presence of famous and expensive movie stars, grandiose sets and costuming, lavish use of extras in crowds and battles, impressive technological effects. Such extravagant spectacle was marketed as a major selling point of the historical epics—these were entertainment 'events', impressive recreations of the grandeur of the ancient world itself.

What becomes of story-telling in such cinema? Does it suffer, as critics claim, from being subordinated to the endless care taken over visual detail and grand display? In everyday thought we associate films primarily with the stories they tell; we would describe *Spartacus* (1960) as a film about the rebellion of the slaves against Rome, and the fate of their leader, or *Titanic* (1997) as a film about the tragic love affair between Jack and Rose on board the doomed ship. But the pleasurable experience of film-going has as much to do with the visual and aural excitement that is the product of styles of filming and of production design. When a tension between spectacle and narrative arises, it is often in large-scale productions such as the historical epics we are discussing, although the western and the musical were also affected by this problem of excessive 'style'. When today's blockbuster action movies are criticised for allowing visual effects to dominate over story-telling it is often seen as a sign of the decline of the values of old-fashioned craftsmanship in the new Hollywood.

Filmic versions of ancient Rome are a convenient focus for an exploration of such tension. The examples I have chosen from the period between 1959 and 1964 all address the problem head-on, and are more or less successful in blending story-telling with spectacle. On the whole this involves a critique (implicit or explicit) of Rome itself as obsessed with the very spectacles we as cinema-goers also enjoy. As an example of this one need only think of Spartacus' disgust at his fellow slaves forcing Romans to fight in an improvised gladiatorial show: 'What are we—Romans?' he exclaims. We find this stance again in *Gladiator*. Maximus' famous 'Are you not entertained?' outburst in the arena confronts the spectator directly with his or her role as a kind of 'Roman'. It seems that at the movies we all have the potential to be Romans, as Michael Wood has pointed out in a much-quoted analysis:

> All these stories invite our sympathy for the oppressed, of course—all the more so because we know that by generously backing these losers we shall find we have backed winners in the end. But then the movies, themselves, as costly studio productions, plainly take the other side. . . . they are all for tyranny and Rome, more imperialist than the emperor. The great scenes in these films, the reasons for our being in the cinema at all—the

orgies, the triumphs, the gladiatorial games—all belong
to the oppressors. The palaces, the costumes, the pomp—
'every conceivable production value' as Selznick said—are
all theirs. It is the Romans who provide the circuses, who
give us a Rome to be gaudily burned.[1]

In art cinema, things tend to be a little more complex. Spectacle and visual pleasure can be undermined or parodied as part
of a tendency to break down the illusions of realism cultivated
by Hollywood in the 1940s, 1950s, and 1960s.[2] *Fellini Satyricon*
offers a good case-study of this approach: the Romans still provide the circuses, so to speak, but visual pleasure is scarce and
we are often repelled rather than fascinated by the orgies and
the games. In *Titus* we come face to face with the consequences
of the use of violence as entertainment when the Colosseum
becomes the stage for a brutal cycle of revenge.

What all six films discussed in this book have in common is
that they are 'historical' in the broadest sense of the word. All
six make use of the cinematic medium to evoke a past world
and past events, the first four with the aim of creating a realistic
experience of it, the final two with the aim of making us question
the differences between past and present, and the validity of our
perceptions of the past. Realism or verisimilitude—the extent
to which the past as presented on the screen is persuasive or
believable—plays a big part in any historical film.[3] This is not
always the same as authenticity; as is well known, authentic
details are often researched but discarded by the producers of
historical films in search of the more visually impressive effect.
In avant-garde or independent film, realism is undermined
precisely in order to disrupt the uncritical absorption that is one
of the great pleasures and attractions of mainstream historical
film. For Robert Rosenstone, whose work on film and history

has been extremely influential, this absorption is a crucial factor in the effectiveness of history on the screen:

> more easily than the written word, the motion picture seems to let us stare through a window directly at past events, to experience people and places as if we were there. The huge images on the screen and the wraparound sounds overwhelm us, swamp our senses, and destroy attempts to remain aloof, distanced, critical. In the movie theater, we are, for a time, prisoners of history.[4]

Rosenstone's evocative description alerts us to a number of features of historical films. First is the illusion created in historical films (as in other mainstream films) that what we are seeing is uncontrived and that we happen upon it as though looking through a window into the past. The creation of such realism is at the heart of the persuasiveness and the aesthetic appeal of all mainstream film; in historical films it is perhaps even more crucial than elsewhere. Second, Rosenstone points out the power of the visual and aural experience of cinema, and the ways in which cinematic technology assaults our senses and pulls us into the world of the film. The lure of the sensory experience of film is such that, according to Rosenstone, our critical (historical) faculties are suspended. That is the third important feature of such films, and it is the most difficult to pin down. Overwhelming spectacular effects can be both alluring and repellent, they can draw us into the world of the cinema and at the same time propel us out of it. Such cinema can, as Rosenstone suggests, take us prisoner. However, it can also increase our awareness of the theatricality and thus of the coerciveness of what we see, and make us uncomfortable with the visual excess displayed on the screen. Historical epics almost always teeter on the edge of the excess of visual spectacle that threatens to overwhelm narrative coherence as they reach for the ultimate aim of verisimilitude. This, according to the influential French film critic André Bazin, is cinema's guiding myth: the 'recreation of the world in its own image'.[5]

Bazin believed that cinema should always aim to fulfil its potential for complete realism, conceived as a world that unfolds before our eyes, unaware of the spectator. There were those, as we shall see, who from the beginning viewed cinema as an art that had to aim to be as far as possible from merely reproducing reality. In this model of cinema the screen acts as a frame rather than a window. Within this frame, a work of art is created, using the techniques of the moving image, perhaps to tell a story, perhaps to *not* tell a story. The viewer must be aware at all times of the difference between screen and reality and of the artifice of what appears on the screen. In the frame, what we see is consciously exhibited for us, and we are conscious of our role as spectators.

For historical films the difference is crucial. In the realist scenario, we are looking at versions of ancient Rome that aim to persuade us that we are seeing antiquity 'as it really was'. What we are being shown on the screen intends to convince us of its historicity. This is problematic, however, as historical film must always be 'staged', i.e. be costumed in historical clothes, make use of reconstructed sets, and so on. The visible artifice of all this is difficult to overcome in any way that would seem acceptably realistic to Bazin himself. Mainstream cinema aims instead to achieve the *illusion* of realism by inviting us to be absorbed in the visual pleasure of cinema as Rosenstone describes it in the passage quoted above. In the second scenario, where artifice and construction are highlighted, we are openly aware of the fact that the past cannot be brought back to life, and that what we are confronted with are interpretations and fictions. We experience a sense of distance, sometimes even alienation from what is presented on the screen, and this makes absorption impossible. Rosenstone's discussion presupposes that there are some fairly constant dividing lines between mainstream cinema and art cinema. In the early twenty-first century such divisions are not as rigid as they once were, with many mainstream directors borrowing from the techniques of the art film. Both *Gladiator* and *Titus*, for instance, contain sequences of deliberately unrealistic imagery that allude to techniques used in music videos. In both cases such sequences break out of the narrative and create a sense of awareness of cinema as an art form.

In Chapter 1 I have given an outline of the key questions and issues that underlie my approach to this material. Beginning with the distinction between artifice and realism that underpins most theoretical treatments of cinema, I discuss the implications of film's connection to narrative, and then the range of ways in which the concepts of narrative, realism, and spectacle are connected. In the four subsequent chapters I examine in more detail the story-telling and the visual style of my four examples of mainstream historical epic. In each chapter I focus first on the film's beginning and ending. This allows me to go into some detail in analysing—in some cases scene by scene—the way in which the films construct their narratives, through both word and image. The beginning of a 'well-made' film, in the classical Hollywood style, is the place where characters and locations are established and explained. As a rule of thumb, it is fair to say that in most conventional films this 'set-up' takes place in the first twenty minutes.[6] The end, in any conventional narrative structure, is where conflict is resolved, questions are answered and loose ends tied up—a good place to examine what a film's message to its viewers really is. Innovative cinema has, of course, always played fast and loose with these fixed points (as does avant-garde fiction with the literary equivalents).

Contemporary cinema, influenced by the aesthetic of music videos and advertising, and by the increased popularity of the action film, also often dispenses with the 'proper' expositions and resolutions, as well as with traditional forms of editing. But the three older films we examine are still very much crafted in a tradition of clear narration, and *Gladiator*, though owing much to the newer aesthetic, is also a film that is keen to tell a good story, and to tell it with some clarity. For each of these four examples I conclude by examining aspects of spectacle and display. What do they display, and why? How complicated is the relationship between narrative and spectacle? We look at the display of the city of Rome itself, at uses of the arena and of violence, at the ways in which the films display landscape and the body.

The final two chapters forgo this pattern because both Fellini's and Taymor's films are more complex and suggestive works of art that reject the principle of the well-told story and illusionist or realist uses of spectacle we find in mainstream films. *Satyricon* and *Titus* are, to a large extent, characterised by the overt or self-aware nature of their artifice. Fellini and Taymor are interested in complicating both our idea of Roman antiquity and our idea of cinema. Both present us with the possibility of a rather challenging and complex way of telling stories and contemplating the past on screen. Both bring spectacle into the foreground, and ensure that the spectator is distanced and reflective, rather than absorbed. But both also create visually original and creative interpretations of ancient Rome and its people and spectacles. In *Satyricon* and in *Titus* Rome is imbued with its literary and artistic history but also with its cinematic history. They are thus films that are both about Rome and about cinematic Rome.

CHAPTER 1

NARRATIVE AND SPECTACLE,
REALISM AND ILLUSION,
AND THE HISTORICAL FILM

Realism and formalism: film as art

A brief discussion of film theory's negotiation of the relationship between image and reality may help to illuminate some of the ways in which screening the past is bound up with a continuing negotiation of realism and technique. Because of its potential for capturing or documenting reality, cinema had to struggle, in its initial stages, to be accepted as an art form. The two early schools of thought that dominate film theory (and practice) until the 1960s both aimed to establish the artistic value of cinema; they also shared the fundamental supposition that cinema is based on the photographic process and must therefore be assessed with a view to its relationship to reality. The Realists (for whom Siegfried Kracauer and André Bazin were prominent representatives) appreciated cinema's ability to provide an exact reproduction of reality as its foremost value. If it could achieve this, cinema would present to the viewer a form of 'reality' that enabled free observation and criticism, instead of manipulating the viewer in the manner of more 'constructed' cinema. For Kracauer, 'film is essentially an extension of photography', and 'films come into their own when they record and reveal physical reality'.[1] The idea that reality is 'revealed' by the camera was crucial to Kracauer's notion of film.[2]

By contrast, the Formalists (including Rudolf Arnheim, Sergei Eisenstein, and Béla Balász) focused on the difference between our empirical perception of the world and the perception of the world in film. In Arnheim's view, cinema had the power to transform reality, and so to produce meaning *beyond* the reality of the photographed image. Arnheim argued that film uses techniques such as lighting, framing, editing, contrast, and repetition to achieve its own shaped or constructed form of reality. In this way film created art, rather than documentation. (Arnheim was very much against the introduction of sound to film, which he saw as a step towards using film as a mere documentary medium.) The filmmaker did not need to document reality, but could tell his or her own version of it and could literally turn reality on its head. Arnheim's vision of what film could do is entirely contrary to the governing principles of realistic story-telling that we encounter in mainstream film. In this theory the ideal filmmaker:

> creates new realities, in which things can be multiplied, turns their movements and actions backward, distorts them, retards or accelerates them. He calls into existence magical worlds where the force of gravity disappears, mysterious powers move inanimate objects, and broken things are made whole. He brings into being symbolic bridges between events and objects that have had no connection in reality.[3]

What Arnheim describes is a style of filming and editing film that highlights the differences between empirical perception ('seeing for oneself') and the transformed reality of the cinema. According to such theories, a cinema that could make the familiar strange could provoke serious political debate, even revolutionise consciousness; this approach can be seen in the films of Sergei Eisenstein.[4]

In the 1960s the basic supposition shared by Formalists and Realists began to be dismantled when it became clear that film needed to be studied as something that was more than a reflection or representation of reality. In mainstream practice it was evident that the line between realism and formalism was not as clear as it had appeared to the early theorists of cinema. In avant-garde practice, movements such as the French Nouvelle Vague and Italian Neorealism redefined cinematic realism to include both documentary-like fidelity to 'real life', and the possibility of more subjective and stylised modes of filming. At the same time, during the 1960s, film theory engaged in the semiotic and narrative analysis of film. The intricacies of the theoretical developments over this period are beyond the scope of this book. Summed up very brutally: film theory arrived finally at a position that refuted any connection between the image shown on screen and the objects that were recorded in order to achieve that image. The point of studying film was no longer the exploration of the medium's relationship to empirical reality, but its potential as a language in its own right. As a consequence of this development, realism could now also be understood as an effect produced by the art of film, and specifically by the way in which film told its stories.[5] This approach is particularly associated with Colin MacCabe, who analysed the way in which film uses narration and point of view to create the illusion that stories almost tell themselves, that the narration is invisible, or, as it came to be described, 'transparent'.[6]

The illusion of reality and transparent narration

Even in the documentary genre, it is now generally acknow-
ledged that film is always in the business of constructing a
representation of reality, and that the language of film can never
be completely neutral or transparent. Nonetheless, spectators of
mainstream Hollywood genres are often enticed to overlook the
tools of construction—such as the scripted dialogue, editing,
sets, lighting and so on—in order to perceive the world on the
screen as natural rather than artificial. This 'overlooking' of the
language of film is achieved in mainstream narrative cinema by
what is often referred to as 'transparent narration'. The point
of this is to create the illusion that what is seen on the screen
is simply there, captured by cameras that just happen to be
there.[7] Narrative itself becomes crucial to the way in which film
ensures that the spectator's illusion of witnessing a continuous
and real unedited event is maintained. The conventions of
'continuity editing', which concern the way in which we perceive
characters in film moving in space and time, are effectively
rules for unobtrusive narration. They include, for instance, the
180-degree rule—how the camera has to position itself in a
way that mimics, in a sense, the 'natural' perception of events
by an observer. David Bordwell explains why the principles of
continuity are so important:

> they assure that the spectator understands how the
> story moves around in space and time. Establishing and
> re-establishing shots situate the actors in the locale. An
> axis of action (or '180-degree line') governs the actors'
> orientation and eyelines, and the shots, however different
> in angle are taken from one side of that axis. The actors'
> movements are matched across cuts, and typically the
> closest shots are reserved for the most significant facial
> reactions and lines of dialogue.[8]

Under this regime, or using this 'language', events, objects, and people on the screen do not exhibit themselves to the viewer; continuity editing makes it feel as though we are catching them unawares. Accordingly, actors in mainstream film cannot show any awareness of the camera—the 180-degree line effectively acts as a fourth wall across which there can be no communication. Talking straight into the camera as is sometimes seen in art film (it occurs in *Satyricon* and in *Titus*) is a clear way to break the illusion of 'filmed reality' created by the unobtrusive camerawork of mainstream Hollywood films. Much like the realist novel of the nineteenth century, with its invisible but all-knowing narrator, realist films aim to create plausible worlds that the camera appears to 'capture' for the audience as though it were documenting real events. In the role of the narrator, the camera's purpose in this story-telling is to present to the viewer the 'right' sort of things in the 'right' sort of order.

In art cinema (and in some contemporary mainstream cinema) the act of narration can of course be far more overt. Indeed, as Bordwell points out, the author or director of such works frequently intrudes into the film, making his or her control over the narration felt.[9] Bordwell's examples of this kind of intrusion include the flash-forward—when a future action is anticipated by the narration before it can logically have taken place. The knowledge needed to tell the story in this order is not available to any character in it, therefore the narrator's presence is necessary and self-conscious and the act of narration is anything but invisible.

As new filming techniques have begun to establish themselves since the end of the studio era, the older style of transparent or unobtrusive narration, evident for the most part in *The Fall of the Roman Empire* (1964) for instance, has gradually given way to a rather more flamboyant style of film editing, which is often more inclined to 'show off' the powers of the medium. This trend is not limited to mainstream film, in fact it borrows some of its characteristic features from art film, as well as from the music video. David Bordwell has conducted a thorough analysis of the style and narration of modern films. The features he lists as contributing to the now dominant style of mainstream filmmaking include: the increased use of the long lens, with its ability to pick out detail; the new digital editing techniques that allow extremely short cuts; the customary use of the steadicam, and of sky or crane shots (these can all be seen in *Gladiator* and in *Titus*). Unlike the transparent narration of older cinema, such techniques draw the spectator's attention to the camera's narration.[10] But this is not an all-out revolution. Bordwell, whose term for the trend is 'intensified continuity', argues that contemporary mainstream films still generally respect the continuities of time and space, but they are also 'more willing to create gaps and inconsistencies, and they strive to make the viewer appreciate their cunning artifice'.[11]

Does this mean that as modern viewers we are also more aware of the language of film, and of the ways in which cinema is able to manipulate and construct its own reality? When we look at Ridley Scott's recreated Rome do we see it as artifice, and are we aware of the spectacular stylishness that characterises it? Does this mean that we are less inclined to believe in its verisimilitude? Do we understand more clearly now than we did in the 1960s that what is presented to us on the screen is only a version of the past created by the art of cinema?

Fact, fiction, and narration in historiography: the idea of 'metahistory'

The scrutiny of cinematic realism, and of film as a means of recording reality, resulted in the blurring of the distinction between fact and fiction. A similar movement can be observed in the analysis of historiography (the writing of history) itself. With the publication in 1973 of the historian Hayden White's book *Metahistory*, it became clear that historiography was never a mere recording of events, but involved plot and narrative, as well as figures or 'tropes' such as metaphor or irony. History, in other words, had to be told as a story in order to make sense. It could also be analysed, just like literature, in terms of its structures and tropes. In a later book, *The Content of the Form*, White argues that in order to be accepted as history, accounts of past events must be shaped in the form of narrative:

> But by common consent, it is not enough that an historical account deal in real, rather than merely imaginary, events; and it is not enough that the account represents events ... according to the chronological sequence in which they originally occurred. The events must be not only registered within the chronological framework of their original occurrence, but narrated as well, that is to say, revealed as possessing a structure, and order of meaning, that they do not possess as a mere sequence.[12]

If we accept the position that narrative is central to the art of history, then the distinctions between the various forms of historical representation (historical novels, paintings, and films) cease to be so clear. As Maria Wyke has shown, cinema itself has its origins in nineteenth-century realist forms of representation, as well as drawing substantially on the nineteenth- and early twentieth-century novel and realist historiography.[13] If all history involves story-telling, the history told in films or novels may have the same status as the ostensibly more 'factual' account given in an academic historical text. The difference is that the historical textbook *appears* not to narrate, for instance by using a neutral or unobtrusive authorial voice. Like the transparent narration of Hollywood film, this is still narration—it is only concealed to invite the reader to disregard it.

Why do narratives need to conceal their story-telling? How does the need for the pretence of objectivity or recording arise? For White, these are crucial questions to ask of historiographical writing. His contention is, very simply put, that narrative is an underlying and trans-cultural mode of communication, that it is part of being human.[14] According to White, narrative becomes a problem in historiography when the distinction is made between mythic or fictional and 'real' events. Narrative may be appropriate for myth and fiction, but real events should not need to be turned into a story. Why can they not just 'tell themselves'? Here White introduces the telling distinction between history that narrates and history that 'narrativises'. When it narrates, according to White, historical discourse is open about the perspective it adopts in reporting events; in other words, the historian makes no secret of his role and his presence as narrator. Narrativising, however, involves a certain amount of subterfuge in creating a seemingly objective point of view: in such writing, the narrator hides away and the writing 'feigns to make the world speak itself and speak itself as a story'.[15] The appearance of objectivity is down to the seeming absence of a narrator. Applying this mode of analysis to film, we can see how 'transparent narration' is a way of concealing the fact of narration while making it appear as though the world on the screen reveals itself, and reveals itself as a story.

Film and narrative

A film's main characters, all agree, should pursue important goals and face forbidding obstacles. Conflict should be constant, across the whole film, and within each scene. Actions should be bound into a tight chain of cause and effect. Major events should be foreshadowed ('planted'), but not so obviously that the viewer can predict them. Tension should rise in the course of the film until a climax resolves all the issues.[16]

Bordwell's summary of the rules that govern Hollywood screenwriting effectively describes the way in which mainstream films tell their stories. In addition, this following extract from a scriptwriter's manual illuminates the principles of cohesion and clarity that govern such narratives and go hand in hand with the idea of transparent narration we have discussed already:

Care must be taken ... that every coincidence is sufficiently motivated to make it credible; that there is no conflict between what has gone on before, what is going on currently; and what will happen in the future; ... that no baffling question marks are left over at the end of the picture to detract from the audience's appreciation of it.[17]

By contrast, life itself is of course full of baffling question marks and unplugged holes—not unlike, for instance *Satyricon*. The paradox of realistic cinema seems to be that in order to present a plausible story in a coherent world, it must rely on a narrative in which all conflict, all questioning, and all self-awareness is erased. It also relies on clearly delineated characters to drive the plot through their ambitions or goals, or through their own psychological journey. In historical drama this form of story-telling may be criticised by historians for failing to address the full range of the complexity and open-endedness of historical events.

In his recent book *History on Film/Film on History*, Robert Rosenstone has a clear and useful analysis of mainstream historical drama, of the role of narration that is at the heart of such films, and of the potential limitations that this imposes on the medium.[18] I paraphrase briefly here the six elements Rosenstone lists. First, he says that the historical feature film tells a story, which is embedded in a wider perspective (usually progressive) of historical events—even when the story itself ends pessimistically. Second, history in such films is always the story of individuals, never of the masses. Third, past events portrayed on the screen in mainstream drama are completed and closed, and their interpretation is clear and unambiguous— there are no loose ends. Fourth, the past is dramatised and 'emotionalised', and the power of the cinematic medium is used to create the impression for the spectator that she or he is experiencing rather than watching events. Fifth, film is able to create a sense of the 'look' of the past through the use of landscape, buildings, dress, and objects, as well as the human body. Finally, Rosenstone says that rather than analyse events and separate them into categories (e.g. social, military, or political history), film shows history as a 'process'. Politics or gender, for instance, are not categories or themes for analysis, but simply form a part of events in history. So historical drama does not discuss, say, the status of women in ancient Egypt, but it might show it through the kinds of things that women do, say, or wear in a film.

What Rosenstone describes, in essence, is how historical films tell stories: by shaping events into narratives, by establishing closure, by finding or inventing protagonists who in turn provide emotional involvement or empathy, and by finding and inventing plausible locales for the narrative. Perhaps the most salient characteristic of such films is the way in which they represent history always as the history of individuals, and historical events as caused by or at least as affecting *only* individuals. It is fairly evident to even the most casual observer, that a goal-oriented protagonist is one of the main distinguishing features of mainstream US film. Such protagonists also form the cornerstone of the narratives of historical feature films; as Rosenstone points out, the story must belong to an individual, not to an anonymous group of people. A good recent example of how historical drama structures history into narrative is *Saving Private Ryan* (1998), directed by Steven Spielberg. Here, the shock of the very powerful opening scene, a vivid and by all accounts very authentic representation of the D-Day landings in Normandy, filmed in a quasi-documentary style, is mitigated very quickly by the development of the story of Private Ryan and his mother. The film is swiftly pulled back from France, and its emotional heart and the core of its narrative located firmly in the USA. Historical events in Europe then become motivated for the viewer by the need to conclude a story about a specific American family. In this way, the vastness of the historical subject becomes manageable; it is a mainstream film focused on an individual's story—not the story of the aftermath of the D-Day landings, but the story of Private Ryan.

Historical narrative and the epic protagonist

Frequently in historical drama (as in the western, and more recently in action adventures and thrillers, too) the protagonist is an outsider in some way, not fully incorporated in an institution or organisation. Being at a distance from institutional power and the corruption that accompanies it, such protagonists are more easily identifiable as individuals with whom the spectator can identify. The lone hero struggling against an establishment or big organisation is a vital ingredient of American popular films, not just in the epics and westerns of classic Hollywood, but in 'new Hollywood' as well. One thinks of the *Terminator* films, and also films such as *The Insider* (1999) and *Erin Brockovich* (2000). Where the protagonist is a policeman, he usually works on the margins of the institution, often exposing corruption, or incompetence, at its core. In *The Patriot* (2000) the protagonist joins the army as a reluctant and idiosyncratic leader in the war against the English.

In historical film it is especially important to keep the protagonist from being fully identified with the institutions and politics of the past. Such identification would tend to highlight the difference between past and present, rather than dwell on the more 'universal' aspect of humanity, and indeed the presence of the human body itself. (Of course, this statement ignores, as does much historical film, the significant differences between past and present human beings, even in their physical appearance. Aspects such as dental hygiene, average size, and even accent are frequently if not always subordinated to historical drama's aim of bringing the past to life.) Still, the centring on an individual without evident ties to political or social institutions is important to Roman history films especially, with their focus on narratives of oppression. The protagonists of *Spartacus*, *Ben-Hur*, *The Fall of the Roman Empire*, and *Gladiator* are all able to represent the oppressed and to establish alternative modes of power, and masculinity. As outsiders they stand for individual freedom and thus allude to, or actually undergo, processes of enlightenment or conversion. This happens to Spartacus as he attains humanity and civilisation instead of his animalistic status at the beginning, to Judah Ben-Hur in his near-conversion to Christianity, to Livius when he turns his back on Roman politics, and to Maximus, whose ultimate aim is liberation in the after-life. In all our examples there is much help for the spectator in building up the salient characteristics of the protagonist to ensure he is at all times 'legible', that his motivation and psychology are always to hand to help the spectator's comprehension of and engagement with the plot. Recurrent motifs are often used to help with this (for instance the giving of water in *Ben-Hur*, or Maximus' handfuls of soil in *Gladiator*).

To see how central such protagonists are, especially in contemporary cinema, and how interlinked their existence is with story-telling in such films, one need only take a look at the advertising slogan for *Gladiator*. To lure an audience back to the cinema to see a historical epic, the story is told here purely as the story of an individual, with no reference made to the historical theme, or to the spectacle that awaits the viewer. The words 'slave', 'gladiator', and 'empire' of course establish, roughly, a sense that this is a story set in ancient Rome—but what matters initially is the individual: 'The general who became a slave. The slave who became a gladiator. The gladiator who defeated an empire'.

By contrast, avant-garde or innovative cinema mostly avoids the use of strong individual protagonists. Characters in art cinema tend merely to observe events and to be affected by them, rather than affect events themselves in the way that the mainstream protagonist does.[19] Encolpio in *Satyricon* is an excellent example of a more or less passive protagonist. He drifts through life and through the film without any clear purpose, apart from curing his temporary erectile dysfunction. In *Titus* the protagonist is unsympathetic to start with and ultimately not capable of triumph over adversity. He is also bound too deeply into an alien code of conduct, which makes it hard to identify with him. Innovative historical drama (starting with Eisenstein perhaps) often represents history as the story of masses of people rather than named individuals. This can help to produce a (perhaps more realistic) sense of disorientation or lack of understanding by the spectator,[20] but disorientation is not desirable in mainstream historical drama, where the stories told about the past must be crystal clear.

Widescreen history, spectacle and realism

As is well-known, CinemaScope and other widescreen techniques had an immediate affinity with historical films, which were among the first to be shown using the new techniques. Historical epic is often linked with the use of the most advanced technology available, and thus becomes a historical event in its own right. When it was first available, however, widescreen technology appeared to Bazin and others to promise the possibility of a more 'honest' realism. Theorists and practitioners anticipated that the wider screen might allow for less editing and cutting so that more action could be perceived simultaneously, as it would be in 'real life'—another case of ideal unobtrusive narration. Consequently there was a great deal of enthusiasm for the potential of this 'modern miracle', as CinemaScope was dubbed in advertising campaigns for *The Robe* (1953). In Bazin's view, all new developments in cinematic technology were driven by the ambition to fulfil his ideal of total verisimilitude. When he came to consider the merits of CinemaScope as a means to achieving this goal (quite apart from its current use in historical spectaculars), Bazin expressed his hopes for the technology in quite utopian terms:

> Film will thus grow even more apart from the abstractions of music and painting, and will get even nearer to its profound vocation, which is to show before it expresses, or, more accurately, to express through the evidence of the real. Put yet another way: the cinema's ultimate aim should be not so much to mean as to reveal.[21]

Similarly, in an analysis of the advantages of CinemaScope, written just ten years after its first use, the critic Charles Barr showed how the availability of this new field of vision might affect the viewer:

> We are left 'free' to interpret the scene visually, and this means we are free to respond. Our responses are not 'signposted' by successive close-ups . . . No single reading of the scene is imposed. One could put it another way: the scene, as directed, is at once more subtle and more *authentic*.[22]

The subtlety and authenticity praised here by Barr result from the relative inactivity of the camera as a narrator. Like Bazin, Barr favoured film as a medium for reporting or presenting reality rather than as a medium for art and fiction. Another early enthusiast for CinemaScope was the famous French cultural critic Roland Barthes, whose comments on the potential of the wide screen are not especially well known, but rather illuminating:

> Up until now, the look of the spectator has been that of someone lying prone and buried, walled up in the darkness, receiving cinematic nourishment rather like the way a patient is fed intravenously. Here the position is totally different: I am on an enormous balcony, I move effortlessly within the field's range, I freely pick out what interests me.[23]

As for Barr, for Barthes the potential for active spectatorship rather than passive consumption was an important development. But Barthes was also especially interested in the potential of the technology for the representation of history:

> Properly speaking, this should be the space of History, and technically, the epical dimension is born. Imagine

yourself in front of *The Battleship Potemkin*, no longer
stationed at the end of a telescope but supported by
the same air, the same stone, the same crowd: this ideal
Potemkin, where you could finally join hands with the
insurgents, share the same light, and experience the
tragic Odessa Steps in their fullest force, this is what
is now possible; the balcony of History is ready. What
remains to be seen is what we'll be shown there; if it will
be *Potemkin* or *The Robe*, Odessa or Saint-Sulpice, History
or Mythology.[24]

Historical fiction such as that shown in *The Robe* did not, for
Barthes, fulfil the potential of the new technology. Like the church
of St Sulpice, with its bourgeois spectacle,[25] *The Robe* stands for
made-up history and a coercive and overpowering dishonest
aesthetic—the very opposite of what CinemaScope *could* achieve
for the cinema. Despite his dissatisfaction with *The Robe*, it is clear
that Barthes identified two potential key virtues of widescreen
projection: the immediacy of its realism ('supported by the
same air, the same stone, the same crowd') and the illusion of
participation and empowerment it created ('I move effortlessly',
'I pick freely', 'join hands with the insurgents'). Both effects are
especially potent when it is the *past* that is brought to life on
the screen. Barthes' notion of a 'balcony' on history evokes the
dream of a complete realism, a cinema that does not look upon
the past from a distance, but immerses the spectator in it.

That was the theory and the propaganda surrounding the
widescreen technology. In fact, the desired increase in realism
is marred (as Barthes recognised) by the bloated spectacle that
accompanies it. The natural participation from the balcony of
history that widescreen projection may appear to invite is made
impossible by the theatricality of the productions. Like previous
technological innovations, the wide screen was also associated,

through the studios' rhetoric and advertising, with luxury, with an excess of spectacle, and certainly with artifice rather than reality.[26]

In the same way, much of the rhetoric surrounding historical films draws attention to the scholarly research that has gone into creating a realistic or 'authentic' experience, while at the same time constantly highlighting the sheer scale of the undertaking, and the excesses that have gone into it.[27] The *effect* of reality, the result of lavish research and expenditure, is displayed to such an extent in the historical epic that it becomes part of the *raison d'être* of such films. Indeed, this spotlighting of spectacle is one of the defining characteristics of the genre. Steve Neale's analysis of historical spectacle points out the interconnection of recreation, realism, spectacular display, and the telling of 'big' stories:

> In the epic, these moments are part of an overall process in which cinema displays itself and its powers through the recreation of a past so distant that much of its impact derives simply from the evidence of the scale of re-creation involved (from details of costume and décor to the construction of whole cities) and through the telling of a story felt to match that scale, such as the story of Christ, the fall of the Roman Empire, and so on.[28]

Among all this excess it would appear that Bazin's 'evidence of the real' cannot hold much sway. The evidence that matters most in the historical epic is that research and reconstruction took place on a major scale in order to create a world that can *appear* to be real. Such a world is then filmed in a way that helps to confirm the appearance of reality, suppressing as far as possible any trace of exhibitionism or spectacle so that films 'appear to unreel, unsolicited, before the eyes of the spectator'.[29]

Narrative and spectacle

Narrative is not the only force at play in historical epic, nor is narration always transparent in such films. Historical epics do tell stories, but those stories have to compete with other factors in a genre that has perhaps best been defined by Steve Neale as 'the coincidence of historical subject matter and a large scale with the use of new technologies and high production values'.[30]

Technology and production values can at times overwhelm the narrative and emphasis on individuals that are vital to successful mainstream cinema. Today critics of the 'new Hollywood' see it as dominated by expensive special-effect laden 'blockbusters' that pay too much attention to thrilling special effects at the expense of story-telling.[31] While this is often seen as a sign of the decline of traditional Hollywood values, a similar anxiety that spectacle and scale might overpower narrative was already palpable in the 1960s. Film promotion and criticism alike repeatedly turn to this issue. For instance, in quotes published in a promotion leaflet for *Spartacus* in 1967, Kirk Douglas is rather defensive about the film's more spectacular qualities: 'We did not start with plans for slaughter, mayhem and arson on a grand scale and then try to build a story around them ... Fire, blood and water splash across the screen only when they intensify the narrative,' and 'Despite spectacular scenes of beauty, grandeur and bloodshed, the objective of Universal's "Spartacus" ... is characterizations which dominate, rather than highlight, sets and crowds'.[32]

A typical strategy in defence of spectacle is to show that it is justified by the narrative, as Douglas does in these statements. Critics such as Bosley Crowther of the *New York Times* were also keen to keep spectacle in its place. Here William Wyler is praised for achieving the right sort of balance between story and spectacle:

Where the excitement of the picture may appear to be in the great scenes . . . the area of fullest engrossment is the scenes of people meeting face to face—Ben-Hur verbally clashing with Messala, a Roman soldier suddenly looking upon Jesus. Here is where the artistic quality and taste of Mr. Wyler have prevailed to make this a rich and glowing drama that far transcends the bounds of spectacle. His big scenes are brilliant and dramatic—that is unquestionable. There has seldom been anything in movies to compare with this picture's chariot race . . . But the scenes that truly reach you and convey the profound ideas are those that establish the sincerity and credibility of characters.[33]

By contrast, regarding *The Fall of the Roman Empire*, the same reviewer is less convinced, finding that the 'Technicolor spectacles', the 'tableaus', and indeed the sheer size of the film has no 'emotional pull' and that the production sinks under its own weight.[34] For all historical films, the balance between story and spectacle is crucial. The difficulty is that historical credibility can be both underpinned and undermined by the role of spectacle in any given film. On the one hand a film set in ancient Rome has to convince the spectator of the authenticity of its images of Rome, which requires the expensive and technologically sophisticated display of sets, costumes, crowds and the like. On the other hand, it has to tell a convincing story that appears naturally before the camera and sustains the illusion for the viewer that he or she is just looking through a window at a different world. Too much attention paid to display can both disrupt the story-line and upset the transparency of the narrative.

This dichotomy between narrative and spectacle is related to the question of artifice and realism. When film displays its art, rather than hide it in order to let a story 'tell itself' in a realist manner, that spectacle appears to win over narrative. For instance, when in *Titanic* the camera sweeps from above over the entire length of the ship, this interrupts the narrative of Jack and Rose—which we thought we were witnessing unobserved— by drawing our attention to the camera's position as narrator, and to the achievements of the production that brings us this impressive set. This happens because there is no natural point of view within the world of the film from which we could observe the entire length of the ship in this way. Suddenly it is clear that the camera is a narrator who is outside the events in the story. The pretence that the story is 'telling itself', as White put it, is shattered.

A fruitful comparison can be made with another, very different, way of showing off production values. In the 'Triumph' episode in the HBO/BBC *Rome* series, an elaborate and costly spectacle is produced in staging Caesar's triumph. Since this is television, which lends itself in any case to the close-up and fragmentary views more easily accommodated on the small screen, the aim is quite a different one. Great care is taken not to give an overarching view of the event, but to set up the point of view, most likely a child's, as there are a number of shots that indicate that the view is blocked by adults standing in the way. Eventually, it appears that the child is lifted onto the pedestal of a statue to improve the view.[35] At no point do we get the kind of panorama that a camera positioned somewhere less subjective would have offered (as for instance in the triumph scenes in *Gladiator*, in *Ben-Hur*, and in *Fall of the Roman Empire*). The camera's position is that of a spectator in the crowd itself, not of an outside narrator. This is not transparent narration, since the camera position is so self-consciously and openly subjective. But it is successful in not allowing spectacular display to overtake narrative. The events perhaps do not tell themselves, but they appear as they might be seen by someone within the picture. The triumph is integrated into the story as it is experienced by people in that story rather than being staged for the benefit of the television viewer.

The old epics are perhaps more explicit about the complexity of that issue. As we are about to see, *Ben-Hur* critiques its own excess through the development of its protagonist's character, and through the overlaid Christ narrative that continually undermines the 'Roman' spectacle. We will see how *Spartacus* and *Fall* avoid the excess associated with the arena and the circus but they are still part of the 'big feel' aesthetic we associate with ancient Rome at the cinema. However, it is common consensus that *Cleopatra* (1963) fails to a large part because it crumbles under the weight of its own 'production values'; the film is just too big, the excess has taken it over. Cleopatra's parade with hundreds of dancers and on top an enormous sphinx through a ridiculously large forum is an example of how spectacle can take on a life of its own—although arguably the queen's knowing wink at Julius Caesar helps a little. What is new about *Gladiator*'s relationship with spectacle is how excess may no longer be an explicit issue. And yet, we find in *Gladiator*, as in its predecessors, a kind of internal 'voice' that can be seen to question or critique its espousal of the values of the epic 'super spectacle'.[36] *Satyricon* is open about its fascination with the spectacular and makes this into one of its themes. Its agenda is precisely to undermine and poke fun at the epics' solemn negotiation of story and spectacle by showing a world in which narrative makes no sense and spectacle is everything. In the dark world of *Titus*, the arena dominates all and narrative is threatened throughout by spectacular displays of violence. As in *Satyricon* the epics' attempts at balance are shown up to be empty gestures—finally, according to *Titus*, we are all trapped in the Colosseum.

CHAPTER 2

BEN-HUR

'TALE OF THE CHRIST' OR TALE OF ROME?

One of the most distinctive characteristics of historical drama is the opening prologue, most frequently a voice-over, and increasingly in contemporary film also projected on screen. Almost all epics start with this, even if they then move on to more ordinary modes of unobtrusive narration. The main purpose in these opening narratives is to give the story the appearance of historiography. The plot that will eventually unfold and absorb the viewer in the fate of individual characters has to be validated somehow by its historical context. The prologue is almost always characterised by its authority and by a certain finality in its outlook—it makes it clear to the viewer that there can only be one way of interpreting history. Bruce Babington and Peter Evans, who have made a detailed study of such epic prologues, demonstrate that the (almost always male) voice of the prologue narrator, 'intones a forceful, moralising rhetoric usually positioned beyond the flux of events, from a perspective in which competing forces are polarised and destiny clarified'.[1] One of the most famous of these narrations has to be the opening of *Quo Vadis* (1951):

> This is the Appian Way . . . Imperial Rome is the centre of
> the Empire and undisputed master of the world. But with

this power inevitably comes corruption. The individual is at the mercy of the state . . . On a Roman cross in Judaea a man died to make men free; to spread the gospel of Love and Redemption. Soon that humble cross is destined to replace the proud eagles that top the victorious Roman standards. This is the story of that immortal conflict.[2]

Not all Roman or biblical epics make such explicit use of the 'voice of history' (to use Babington and Evans' term) to establish the narrative agenda—but a good number do, as we shall see. In almost all openings of this kind, the point is not only to set the historical scene, but also to offer a historical perspective: 'soon that humble cross is destined to replace . . .'. The perspective we are asked to take is that of the modern viewer who knows how all this will end. This telling of the story with hindsight, or as Rosenstone puts it, with a 'progressive' view of history, is perhaps the most distinctive feature of films set in ancient Rome.

Beginning: 'you're either with me or you're against me'

Most viewers remember the chariot race as the climax of *Ben-Hur* (and consequently think of it as a film about the protagonist's struggle against Messala and Rome. But the film neither begins nor ends with this story. Instead it embeds this 'struggle-against-Rome' plot in the 'tale of the Christ' of the subtitle of Lew Wallace's novel on which the film was based, and of the alternative title by which the movie was distributed in the USA. One ramification of this embedding is that the film's negotiation of its own spectacularity—of the ways in which it offers the viewer the pleasures of spectacle associated with Romans on film—is more complex than it might otherwise be. The film's beginning and end can be seen to undermine the validity of the events in which the viewer becomes absorbed.

Part of what *Ben-Hur* depicts is the rejection of our keen interest in the conventional narrative of struggle and domination and its associated spectacles. The framing narrative of Christ's birth, suffering, and death is vital to an understanding of the kind of story that *Ben-Hur* aims to tell about Rome.

In theatres in 1959 the film began with a lengthy overture (six minutes) that established the film as a major theatrical event before the curtain went up, and put appropriate emphasis on the importance of Miklos Rosza's score. Of course, the overture is lost on today's DVD viewer who will simply skip it—but it ought to be borne in mind as part of the total, and perhaps really 'epic' experience of cinema at the time. After the overture, but before the title credits, the curtain went up to reveal a naive or old-looking map of the region of ancient Judaea, with the words ANNO DOMINI imposed over it; the viewer is thus alerted to time and place, and to the film's historical ambitions. After this, the screen displays a pastoral landscape, traversed by long trails of travellers, watched over by Roman soldiers. All this occurs in a shot that exhibits Wyler's trademark 'depth of field', a relatively long shot during which we can observe both the expanse of the landscape on the screen, and plenty of detail (facial features and clothes of individual travellers, animals, the Roman insignia in the foreground and so on). Wyler's framing and camerawork give the filmic space the appearance of a 'real' space in which the story unfolds before an observer who is (almost) part of the picture. The soldiers in red and gold with their backs to the camera and the Roman standards are in the front of the picture, cutting into the spectator's view of the landscape, as they might if one were standing right behind them. This perspective also helps the voice-over narrator sound natural (Finlay Currie, who later appears as Balthasar to try and help Judah find the way to Jesus and was known to movie-goers at the time as St Paul from *Quo Vadis*). He could be standing there, right behind the soldiers and watching the Judaeans walk past, while explaining to us what is happening. The opening voice-over of *The Robe* is perhaps similar in that it is spoken by the protagonist himself as he walks around the market square and observes Roman life.

The prologue, not unlike that of *Quo Vadis*, ensures that we have the correct historical perspective, introducing Rome immediately as the oppressor, by verbally reinforcing the visual clues given by the prominence of the soldiers and standards in the picture ('Judaea, for nearly a century, had lain under the mastery of Rome'), and ensuring that the viewer's sympathies lie with the travelling Jews on their way to Jerusalem ('the troubled heart of their land'). Again, this uses words to support what the camera does visually by following the travellers from a height not much above that of the average person, allowing the viewer to inhabit the space as a sympathetic observer. There follow more overtly didactic shots of the fortress of Antonia with the humble Judaeans going about their business around it, while the narrator tells us that 'even as they obey the will of Caesar' the people hope for the redeemer who will 'bring them salvation and perfect freedom'. The Golden Temple, described as 'the outward sign of an inward and imperishable faith', is not shown to be any less monolithic and domineering than the Roman fortress; the contrast, of course, that is about to be made is that between all such 'outward' monuments and the more humble spirituality that will be found through the shepherds at Bethlehem.

More than that, though, the prologue makes it clear that the expectation of spiritual redemption is linked with the notion of freedom from Rome, and Messianic salvation is set up as the opposite of Roman (earthly) tyranny, in a theme that will find its ultimate resolution in Judah's own near-conversion at the end. This deft move, linking spiritual salvation with freedom from slavery and tyranny, is familiar from the *Quo Vadis* prologue ('Soon that humble cross is destined to replace the proud eagles that top the victorious Roman standards'). We will see that it also forms a strong undercurrent in *Spartacus*—and in *Gladiator* too. But here, in *Ben-Hur*, the rise of Christianity is not a mere backdrop or anticipation: we are intended to view it as the backbone of the story itself. The nativity story that concludes this pre-credits sequence is entirely wordless, underlined only by the rather magnificent score and by the painterly quality of the landscape shots with the star of Bethlehem travelling through the sky and eventually shining on the stable. The nativity is a strange and perhaps incongruous part of the film—not least because it appears stylistically at odds with the vivid realism of the rest of Wyler's film. Maybe this is the point: the realism that we expect and enjoy in a historical film is too bound up with the exhibition of spectacular technological achievement; the nativity should be a more sublime moment.

The juxtaposition of the sound of the *shofar* (a traditional Jewish horn instrument with strong religious associations) played by one of the shepherds outside the stable at Bethlehem with the Roman military fanfare sets the tone at the end of the sequence for the imminent epic conflict between the two civilisations. Now we see the grandiose title credits, in sculpted gold letters over Michelangelo's 'Creation of Man' from the roof of the Sistine Chapel, a visual anachronism that highlights the mixture of humanism and Christianity that dominates the film's message. The image, enlarged to extend across the width of the enormous screen, is also a sign that this film intends to be an event and a story bigger than the revenge narrative that forms its core. The contact between the human and the divine and the act of creation itself are a much bigger picture than the story of the rivalry and hatred between two men, even between two cultures. The use of the image also transports the viewer into the distant past and lends cultural weight and credibility to a story that was known to audiences from numerous earlier theatrical and filmic versions for its spectacular qualities.[3]

After the title credits we return to the pastoral Judaean landscape for another long and deep shot; only this time the figures crossing the screen are Roman soldiers rather than Judaean travellers. But what about our plot and our protagonist? So far, we have no indication (bar the title) of who or what this film will be about, if it is not about Jesus. We learn from a brief exchange that this is Nazareth, and we see Joseph in his workshop, defending his son's apparent eccentricity to a neighbour while the soldiers marching past can be glimpsed from the window. A visual contrast is then set up between Jesus, a solitary figure seen from afar, walking in the hills, and the entry of the Roman military machine into Jerusalem under Messala's command.

So far the plot is composed around the opposition between the figure of Jesus embedded in the landscape and the presence and control exerted by Rome. When the camera finally settles on Messala as a protagonist, his first words confirm this impression. With just a hint of psychological instability in the smile he suppresses, Stephen Boyd's Messala announces the fulfilment of his boyhood dreams: 'Now I am in command!' But the degree of control he actually has begins to be questioned during the initial dialogue with Sextus, the outgoing leader of the legion, who alerts Messala to the problems caused by the Messiah and his followers. Messala's lack of understanding for the spiritual movement Sextus describes is then linked explicitly to his reverence for the emperor ('There is divinity in only one man. The emperor is displeased') and to his own tyranny over others ('Punish them. Find the leaders'). In this way the link made in the prologue between Christianity and the release from Roman tyranny is established not merely as historical perspective but becomes part of the plot itself.

The two extraordinary scenes between Charlton Heston and Stephen Boyd that follow this introduction serve to establish our real protagonist and the central plot. The first view we get of Judah Ben-Hur is once more a characteristically deep shot: Charlton Heston's unmistakable monolithic figure framed by a doorway at the very end of the set, first immobile, then running towards his friend. The reunion of the two friends is the start of ten powerfully dramatic minutes in which the screen is dominated almost exclusively by the two men, shot mainly from the torso up, in semi close-up. The film has clearly now focused in from the sweeping landscapes and moving masses that set up the historical scene to the human drama that will keep the viewer hooked. The Christian motif is hinted at visually when the two men compete by throwing spears at the crossed beams that dominate the scene. The camera stays on those beams just long enough (twice) to establish the symbolic significance of the cross in the struggle between the protagonists (the playful competition anticipates the later, real, competition). The conflict is established, true to classical form, by the end of the end of the twenty-third minute when Judah has stated his position: 'Withdraw your legions, give us our freedom'. But the camera continues to hold both men in its frame—as though resolution were still possible—for a further eight minutes (during some of this time we are also introduced to Judah's mother and sister).

The second dialogue scene between Judah and Messala brings the final rift that is first spiritual and then political. The camera is on the two men throughout, again mainly on the torso and above. There are several shot-reverse-shot sequences, as one would expect during such a debate. Messala once more displays his love for the tyranny he represents: he smiles and exults as he announces to Judah, 'The emperor is watching us, judging us. All I need do is serve him'. Judah picks up on the implications of this immediately, answering, 'You speak as if he were god'. Messala confirms our worst fears when he answers: 'He is god, the only god. He is power, real power on earth'. And, looking up with a dismissive hand gesture he adds: 'Not—*that*'. In this way, Messala dismisses Judaeo-Christian spirituality and, at the same time, displays his own devotion to the worship of a deified ruler instead of an unidentified spiritual presence. In this way it also becomes clear that Romans themselves are enslaved mentally by the idea of Roman power and that Messala lacks proper humanity in his misguided insistence on subjecting himself to an empire instead of seeking spiritual enlightenment. The politics follows on from this during a very long take (almost one and a half minutes) that shows the hardening of their positions, beginning with Messala's demand for information on the rebels ('Who are they?') and ending, after Judah's refusal to name them, with Messala's contemptuous remark ('In the name of all the gods, Judah, what can the lives of a few Jews mean to you?') The final falling-out, with Messala's famous line, 'You're either with me or against me,' ends with the first close-up shot of Charlton Heston alone, isolated now as our true protagonist.

In this set-up of just thirty minutes (including the overture) Wyler has cannily exploited the full potential of the wide screen for immediate and naturalistic realism (through the depth of field of the big landscape scenes as well as in the scenes in Judah's house and garden) and drawn the viewer into a story that appears to 'tell itself' as the screen invites us to watch events unfolding, without drawing much attention to the camera. He has also established a human conflict right at the centre of this big historical epic. For ten minutes we have watched the intense drama of the conflict between Messala and Judah unfold and become the focus of the story. Three important plot elements have emerged. Politically, Rome is the oppressor, and the potential for change or uprising is established. Spiritually, there is an underlying (for the moment) narrative of anticipated salvation and possible conversion. And, personally, Messala is already morally corrupt and a reconciliation between him and Judah impossible, as demonstrated by Messala's absolute subjection to the emperor's divinity and power. From these three elements Wyler's film weaves the compelling narrative of enslavement, escape, and retribution that most viewers remember. The climax of this narrative is the chariot race, during which Messala shows his darkest side one last time, and which ends with his defeat and death.

All of this, and also Judah's subsequent discovery of his mother and sister in the leper colony, is overshadowed by the Sermon on the Mount, the crucifixion, and the tentative move towards a conversion of the protagonist that form the final part of the film. At the point where the human conflict between Judah and Messala is resolved and Judah regains his rightful position as a Jewish prince, we are reminded that this, after all, was not what the film was about. We may have been rooting for Judah to take his rightful revenge on Messala and Rome, but the freedom Judah must aim for in this story is a different one.

Missing the Sermon on the Mount (a crisis of masculinity)
Judah's triumph in the arena formally occurs in around the 165th minute of this 214-minute film, and so marks the beginning of the end. About half-way through the film, when Judah has returned to Judaea, the idea of a competition in the arena is first formulated (by the Sheik, who hopes to persuade Judah to race his horses). The Sheik's plan is, significantly, put in direct

opposition with the person of Jesus and a 'path to God', through Balthasar's speech. In this way, the film's narrative is poised at this crucial point between the two opposing paths that have characterised it all along: the circus and God.

It soon becomes clear after Judah's return to his country that there are a number of different avenues to closure. First, the family needs to be reunited, the mother and sister rescued from their suffering. Second, revenge must be exacted on Messala. Third, there is the impetus (formulated by Esther's father) to liberate Judaea from Roman rule. Finally, the path towards salvation is formulated at different stages by Balthasar and by Esther. It is no surprise that the victory in the circus and Messala's death do not, after all, provide an ending, however much they stay in the spectator's mind as the film's narrative and spectacular climax. Ending here would mean that *Ben-Hur* ends on Roman terms— that the world is, indeed, Rome, as Pilate later says to Judah. Instead of the crowning with the laurel wreath that completes the circus sequence, it is the conversion story that provides a tantalising, but ultimately not quite realised, end for the film. Judah's tentative steps on the path towards Christianity form the basis for the final forty-five or fifty minutes—almost a third of the film.

After discovering his mother and sister in the leper colony, Judah narrowly misses hearing the Sermon on the Mount, which the viewer must suspect would have aided him in finding his way. Balthasar tries to persuade him to come, but Judah declares: 'I have business with Rome' before turning his back on Jesus (whom he would have recognised as the man who saved his life earlier in the film). However, when he learns from Pontius Pilate that he has been given Roman citizenship, Judah makes the decision to turn his back on Rome. As at the start of the film, Judah has to choose between Rome and Judaea; returning

Arrius' ring (echoing the removal of Esther's slave ring earlier in the film), he makes his choice. But it appears that he still has some way to go, as Esther points out to him: 'It's as though you have become Messala'.

At this point it seems that the Roman model of violent hyper-masculinity has become the only possible direction for Judah. Esther must provide a way out of this, and set Judah on the proper path towards a more satisfactory ending. Finally, when Judah has been reunited with his mother and sister he takes Esther's advice and attempts to bring them to Jesus: too late, it seems, as they arrive to find Pilate washing his hands. The film is now nearing its end (this is about minute 195). There is a kind of inverted Roman triumph as the camera follows Jesus carrying the cross through the thronged masses in Jerusalem. There are some agonising extreme close-up shots of the cross itself, and of Jesus collapsing under its weight—these camera angles are very effective, and very unlike the techniques used to film Romans. Throughout all this, the face of Jesus is never shown—the reaction shots are all the more important for this. What this scene stresses above all is Judah's own change of perspective—and ours too. It is also striking how much the camera lingers on individual faces and reactions in the crowd (as well as those of the protagonists, of course), thus allowing the spectator a point of view from within the picture, as it were, rather than from a 'historical' perspective.

In this way, Wyler ensures that this final sequence is not the kind of spectacle we associate with 'lavish' biblical epics. He mainly avoids the historical tableau or panorama in favour of the striking close shots in which the bars of the cross or the soldiers' shields literally obstruct our view, with the camera frequently positioned in or very close to the crowd. When Judah finally attempts to give Jesus a drink of water, the exchange of looks between them (which mirrors exactly the similar exchange at the start of the film) disrupts any sense of this sequence as spectacle: the 'gaze' is part of the story here. In looking at Jesus, and in having Jesus look at him, Judah makes one more step towards salvation. Also the exchange of looks, a kind of silent dialogue between the two protagonists, excludes the watching crowds, and counteracts the sense of Jesus' path to the cross as just cinematic spectacle. When Jesus is nailed to the cross, Wyler's stroke of genius is to position the camera (again) right behind and above his head. The angle is striking, and not naturalistic or in any way unobtrusive. At this moment of high drama Wyler is right to deploy a consciously 'artistic' angle that draws attention to the camerawork rather than efface its presence. During the crucifixion sequence, which sees Judah further along his journey towards salvation, there are some very long close-up shots of Charlton Heston's face, and these monolithic close-ups serve repeatedly to emphasise the position and the responsibility perhaps of the spectator in this picture. In terms of the narrative, it is clear that now as the two protagonists' paths converge and finally part, Judah is well on the way towards salvation—and that this is what the story has all been about.

There follows an epilogue depicting the curing of Miriam and Tirza during the storm that attends Jesus' death on the cross. Wyler films this very effectively, and again in a very self-consciously 'artistic' way, intercutting the curing of the two women with brief flashes of Jesus, first a kind of diagonal shot of his body on the cross as the storm begins to rage, and then a close-up of his bleeding hand juxtaposed with Tirza's healed hand. The film's proper finale is the rain, mingled with Jesus' blood, that washes over the screen, a visualisation of the 'rivers of water' which Jesus says will flow from him in John 7:37 (and the water that John says flows from his body, along with blood when the Roman soldier drives a spear into his side). The rivers of water at the end of Wyler's film also anticipate the baptism that Judah will eventually undergo as he is moving towards conversion. It is indicative of Wyler's skill as a filmmaker that he uses these images to tell this story of conversion; of course, water has been the visual symbol that has bound Judah and Christ together since the start of the film.

Transcending the bounds of spectacle?

Does spectacle overwhelm narrative in *Ben-Hur*? The question of the relationship between the two aspects of film is at the heart of much writing on historical epics, as we established in the introduction. The publicity machine around *Ben-Hur* presents it very much as a part of the tradition of big epic spectacles. Everything about it was colossal: it was widely publicised as the most expensive film ever made; its sets were huge and numerous; and the chariot race itself was known to be the most expensive and complex action sequence ever filmed. In addition to such superlatives, the production's location at the Cinecittà studios linked it to a tradition of films made there (*Quo Vadis*, for instance) and to the city of Rome itself. A press-book published in 1959, *The Story of the Making of Ben-Hur*, informs viewers that the set at Cinecittà had become one of the 'historic landmarks with which the Eternal City abounds':

> Typical of thousands of tourists in Rome during this period, you would have boarded a blue-and-white trolley, hopped on a bus or scrambled into a taxi and headed for the plains at the foot of the Alban Hills on the outskirts of the city.
>
> The magnet? . . . Cinecittà Studios where *Ben-Hur* was being filmed.[4]

In addition, the technological achievement of the Camera 65 system was celebrated (as all such contemporary developments in widescreen projection tended to be) as the latest achievement in a realistic and participatory experience of cinema. In the case of Camera 65, the camera itself is something of a monument to the size of the undertaking, and it did feature a fair amount in the publicity for the film. As the first showcasing of MGM's extra-wide 'Ultra Panavision 70' process,[5] *Ben-Hur* is billed on one poster as 'The Entertainment Experience of a Lifetime'. The extremely wide aspect ratio of this process made it especially costly for movie theatres to adjust in order to show the film in road-show engagements, but this would have added to the excitement surrounding the film as an event. *The Story of the Making of Ben-Hur* comments on the technology too:

> The past few years have witnessed many notable advancements in wide-screen filming and projection techniques—all aimed at a greater sense of audience participation in action on the screen. In filming *Ben-Hur*, MGM was determined to have the most exciting photography obtainable. Indeed, the wide sweep and grandeur of its spectacular scenes, as well as the importance of its more intimate scenes, made it mandatory that the most dramatic pictorial method should be used.[6]

It comes as no surprise that among the eleven Academy Awards earned by *Ben-Hur* were Best Visual Effects, Best Sound, and Best Color Cinematography. As a technological event, *Ben-Hur* is best compared with, say, *Titanic*, another historical epic 'blockbuster' with eleven Academy Awards to its name (including Sound, Visual Effects, Cinematography) and a reputation for technological innovation. In the best tradition of such films, *Titanic* was also 'the most expensive film ever made', its technological displays of brilliance matched by the ambition of its historical 'accuracy' (in set design etc.). On the balance between narrative and spectacle in *Titanic* the *New York Times* film reviewer said, 'What a rarity that makes it in today's world of meaningless gimmicks and short attention spans: a huge, thrilling three-and-a-quarter-hour experience that unerringly lures viewers into the beauty and heartbreak of its lost world'.[7] Similarly, for all its technological achievement and monumental status in the history of big historical epics, *Ben-Hur* was celebrated in the press as an 'intimate epic' in which spectacle had not been allowed to overwhelm narrative. Wyler was lauded for his successful depiction of character and human relationships. Contemporary critics felt that William Wyler's background in smaller-scale pictures (and undoubtedly also his reputation, built by André Bazin himself, as a 'serious' director) was a bonus when it came to the direction of *Ben-Hur*.

Next, I will look in some detail at the interaction between narrative and spectacle in the scenes leading up to and including Judah's arrival in Rome on Arrius' triumphal chariot. There is no doubt that Arrius' triumph is 'spectacle' of the type that Steve Neale has described as typical for the genre. As Neale says, such occasions are motivated by the narrative 'quite specifically as displays of power'; they also 'always take place in a narrative context in which they are subject to the controlling gaze of a representative or representatives of whatever ancient state power happens to be the focus of the discursive representation in any particular epic film'.[8] In addition, such spectacles display cinema itself and its achievements (sets, costumes, camera movements, colour and sound, for instance); as Neale has put it, 'these moments are part of an overall process in which cinema displays itself and its powers'.[9]

The triumph is of course a display of power, and it is motivated as such in the film. As is the case with many films about ancient Rome made after 1945, the display of power is also intended to display the analogy between imperial Rome and the fascist regimes of Germany and Italy.[10] But whose power is really on display, and what other factors has Wyler brought into the mix? First, it is clear that Arrius owes his life to Judah's intervention in the aftermath of the naval battle. The triumph is thus at least partly viewed as a celebration of the new relationship between Judah and Arrius that has replaced Judah's poisoned friendship with Messala.

Just minutes before the triumph, we see how Judah saves Arrius from suicide by effectively taking him prisoner—we see him holding on to a chained Arrius to prevent him from throwing himself off the raft. The scene is itself a spectacular display of masculinity, with Charlton Heston's barely clothed body towering over the shackled Arrius. More than that, the inversion of roles—with Arrius now the prisoner—is especially striking after the famous rowing scene in which Judah had been in a very uncomfortable position performing as a classic object of 'the gaze', subjected to Arrius' sadistic and controlling look.[11] Now the body of Charlton Heston is on display once more, but unchained and in control of Arrius. He is also in control of the raft and, by extension, of the ocean that surrounds them. His body viewed in this way, in command of both man and nature, is a very different type of spectacle. For a start, there is no controlling spectator to be seen. The vastness of the sea, covering the expanse of the wide screen, highlights the absence of any spectators and emphasises Arrius' own inability to exert a controlling gaze any more. In saving Arrius from his pagan (and thus misguided) idea of masculinity, which demands his suicide after what he considers his loss of honour, Judah has asserted the validity of a more modern model of masculinity. Seizing power in this way can justify the display of his body at this moment, and perhaps mitigates the discomfort of the previous scene.

Wyler does not intend us to forget that scene below deck. Immediately before the triumph unfolds, we see Judah, now on board a Roman ship with Arrius, gazing down at the galley slaves through a barred trapdoor. The camera angle is from below deck and, filming against the light that comes in through the trapdoor, the screen is dominated by the black outline shadow of a rowing slave's head and torso. Judah and Arrius can just be seen looking in through the bars. This image is faded out, and we are presented with the magnificent panorama of the triumphal procession. But the bars on the trapdoor linger just long enough in the fade-out to remain briefly superimposed on the triumph. With this overt and self-conscious piece of narration, the point about the triumph as a spectacle of oppression is made before the scene even begins.

As Neale points out, the 'controlling gaze' that observes the spectacle is a necessary ingredient to its narrative motivation. Wyler ensures that the viewer is aware, from the moment the scene begins, of the controlling look and presence of the Emperor Tiberius. The first view we have of the triumph is almost as deep as it is wide, shot from behind the set and framed by monumental columns. The parade moves in a long line from the very back of the picture towards the emperor at the front, creating the impression of a vanishing point, or one-point perspective. One reason for this composition is to create an artificial depth that works well to counteract the wide, and always potentially flat, appearance of the 70mm projection. But one-point perspective is rather a blunt instrument, and can appear to be trying to coerce the viewer into accepting its illusion of one central point. Wyler was probably well aware of this, and composed his first view of the triumph in this way in

order to underline the emperor's total control over events, and
emphasise his position as the ultimate spectator (see Fig. 1). This
is not to say, of course, that Wyler had any notion of 'the gaze'
as it is now discussed by film theorists.[12] But the emperor's gaze
as a means of control is present in the script from the start, as
we saw earlier. The breaking point between Messala and Judah
occurs when Messala reveals the quasi-religious passion he has
for the notion that 'the emperor is watching us'. Arrius is not
free, he serves the emperor under whose gaze he performs the
triumph. Messala's fantasy of complete subordination to Roman
power is embodied in the triumph, and so the narrative and the
political points are made. This society uses spectacle to display
power, and it is a society enslaved under the control of those
who produce the spectacles.[13]

The triumph is not only about condemning Roman displays
of power. It does provide Wyler with the opportunity to exploit

1 *The triumph in* Ben-Hur *seen from behind the emperor's throne.*
Image from author's own collection. Copyright: Warner Brothers.

the technology at his disposal in order to create maximal visual pleasure and maximal realism. Thus, the narrative may be asking the viewer to take note of the vertical axis along which the all-seeing, god-like Tiberius is in control, backed by the oversized eagle that supports visually the script's interpretation of the emperor as a totalitarian leader. Wyler alternates this angle with a more liberal exploration of the width of the screen, which succeeds in bringing the splendour of the parade and the excitement of the crowd to life in the most involving way (especially if one imagines seeing it on a big screen). The views of the parade and the crowds across the width of the frame can be described as a display of the power of cinema to bring the past to life. The relatively new widescreen projection was often perceived at the time as offering viewers a new freedom to explore the picture, and thus as giving them a new sense of participation. This Wyler allows in the wider views of the triumph, while restricting it in the more coercive views from behind the emperor's throne. Put very simply, we can see the tension between narrative and spectacle at play in this scene in the conflict between the vertical and the horizontal 'pull' of the picture.[14]

In addition, Wyler is careful to undercut the spectacular panorama with closer reaction shots of Judah, which provide a view of the spectacle through his critical eyes. For instance, when the emperor lifts his finger and the crowd is silenced instantly, the camera cuts to show Judah rather taken aback by the total obedience shown to one man. In reacting independently to the triumph, Judah is also removed from the position of being a part of the Roman display of power, either as a paraded foreign prisoner, or as Arrius' colleague. Either role would subject our protagonist to Tiberius' gaze and to the crowds' enthusiasm for spectacle. Instead, Wyler's direction brings Judah into the foreground as critical observer.

A similar approach is taken in the banquet scene that follows shortly afterwards. Once again a lavish spectacle is provided for the Romans' (and of course the viewers') enjoyment. The scene includes a memorable dance sequence provided by the (uncredited) Ballets Africains, a dance troupe formed in Guinea in 1952 with an expressly pan-African and emancipatory agenda. It seems oddly jarring to see them playing at being Roman dancing slaves in this sequence. Judah observes the extravagant party dispassionately, and also shows little interest in his female companion. As viewers, we have the pleasure of the lavish display, as well as a sense of righteousness derived from sharing Judah's barely concealed contempt for it all. When he finally makes the decision to part with Arrius and return home, we see him looking out at a very pretty night-time view of Rome from a terrace at Arrius' house—another gorgeous spectacle, a view of a city *made* for display. Its effect is undermined because it has no impact on the protagonist. Again, we can enjoy it, but are made aware of the shallowness of its appeal when compared to the deeper values of home and family for which Judah yearns.

The chariot race is, of course, *Ben-Hur*'s most spectacular set piece, and the scene that everyone in 1959 was waiting to see (and to compare with Fred Niblo's 1925 version). The stories surrounding the filming of the sequence were well known at the time, and added to the sense of excitement surrounding the spectacle in the arena. It should be borne in mind, too, that in an era before CGI, some of the excitement surrounding such cinematic events is in the fact that what is seen on screen *actually happened* in some way. The existence of the 'pro-filmic event' is made all the more vivid on the wide screen that captures so much of it at the same time, including shots of the entire arena from a bird's-eye view and panning all round it (not unlike Ridley

Scott's celebrated 360-degree views of his computer-generated Colosseum in *Gladiator*).

The chariot race is not 'pure' spectacle, though. Its narrative motivation is obvious: there has to be a final battle between the two men. The fact that this reckoning takes place in the arena, as an entertainment for the masses and for the Roman elite, is problematic. While it is part of the tradition of such films that a final 'show-down' takes place in some form of arena, it can be awkward to have the protagonist cast as an entertainer. When Judah wins the race he has, in a sense, just won at a game, not in real life. His triumph only takes place in the world of the arena. Many films deal with this problem by somehow blurring the boundaries between the arena and real life. This might be done by creating a situation in which, as in *Quo Vadis*, the protagonist elects to fight in order to rescue the woman he loves, or by show-ing that the protagonist's victory in the arena has immediate effects outside it, or by having the protagonist fight the emperor himself in the arena (as in *Fall* and *Gladiator*). This does not happen in *Ben-Hur*. Despite the fact that Judah succeeds in win-ning the race and mortally wounding Messala, he does not come closer to achieving what he wants (the release of his mother and sister). Neither does he gain any real power outside the arena, as is highlighted by his crowning with the victor's laurel wreath, viewed as a hollow gesture that is part of the empty spectacle.

The chariot race fulfils Neale's description of the role and nature of spectacle in historical epic, but in Wyler's *Ben-Hur* it is also embedded in a discourse of criticism of such spectacle through the narrative, and in particular through the development of Judah's character as a critical observer of the society of spectacle he inhabits. We can conclude that *Ben-Hur* critiques its own spectacularity and shows a nuanced exploitation of the relationship between narrative and spectacle.

CHAPTER 3

SPARTACUS AND THE POLITICS OF STORY-TELLING

―――――――――

'There has never been a great historical film.' So Stanley Kubrick told a pair of interviewers from *Sight and Sound* in 1972. The interview was about *A Clockwork Orange*, but when Kubrick was asked to comment on the progress on his project of a film about Napoleon, he was rather pessimistic. He went on to elaborate:

> I don't think anyone has ever successfully solved the problem of dealing in an interesting way with the historical information that has to be conveyed, and at the same time getting a sense of reality about the daily life of the characters. You have to get a feeling of what it was like to be with Napoleon. At the same time, you have to convey enough historical information in an intelligent, interesting and concise way so that the audience understands what happened.[1]

Kubrick's ambivalence towards the genre can be felt in *Spartacus* (1960), often called 'the thinking man's epic'. It is billed as a great spectacle, with gladiatorial fighting and grand battles; but as we now have it the film shows one battle and one sequence of forced gladiatorial combat—both ending in forms of defeat for the protagonists. It promises to be a film about a legendary character who comes close to causing the fall of

2   Poster for Spartacus. *Image from author's own collection.*
Copyright: Universal.

Rome ('they trained him to kill, but they trained him too well',
as one of the advertising slogans put it), but the story ends in
utter defeat and does not really ever come close to triumph (see
Fig. 2).

Both as spectacle and as narrative, this is a complicated film,
in which a number of different ideas struggle for dominance.[2]
The film's ultimate lack of coherence is probably largely due to
political decisions determining the presentation of Spartacus'
achievement. The story is haunted by the almost complete
absence of success or optimism on the side of the slaves, and
troubled by an oddly assembled middle part in which there is
much political intrigue in Rome and little action between slaves

and Romans. As a spectacle, the film is perhaps the most self-conscious of all historical epics. The display of the male body is at its core, and that is perhaps the only consistent axis around which the two conflicting models of masculinity revolve.[3] Crassus' display of his own power is framed and enhanced by the environments of the baths, the Senate, and his own villas. Spartacus, though trained for display, appears only once as a performer in the arena, at the training school, rather a grim and unspectacular place. Apart from the scenes in the training school, the display of his body and power are almost always framed by nature and landscape, and he is mostly seen in quasi-paternal roles.[4] He is subjected to considerable physical suffering, which is the norm when the male body is centrally displayed in mainstream film. The film has no triumph, no banqueting scene and no crowd-pleasing gladiators in the arena. There are, of course, no Christians in *Spartacus* (though there are crucifixions aplenty). Its most 'spectacular' use of the Super Technirama technology is in the many panoramic landscape shots, and in the memorable battle sequence and its aftermath. But *Spartacus* does not quite achieve the truly innovative treatment of history on film that its director might have wished. In an interview with the *New York Times* in 1960, just before the film's première, Kubrick seemed more optimistic about the film's success than he would be in later life:

> Mr Kubrick feels that he has a film to be taken seriously even by his avant-garde admirers—unlike the usual 'costume epics', none of which he has particularly admired. 'Let's say', he added mildly, 'that I was more influenced by Eisenstein's *Alexander Nevsky*, than by *Ben-Hur*, or anything by Cecil B. DeMille.[5]

Decline and fall again?

Saul Bass's exquisitely designed title sequence for *Spartacus* shows a series of fragments of stone statues—a hand, a jug, a sword, and inscriptions—and ends with a final male bust cracking apart. The use of parts of statues, and the symbolic breaking apart at the conclusion could be interpreted as an allusion to our incomplete knowledge of the ancient world. The stark elegance of the sequence seems designed to prepare the viewer for a more cerebral experience than is usually associated with historical epic. However, the designer himself gives a very different interpretation on an audio commentary of a recent DVD special edition when he states that the opening credits were intended as:

> an evocation of the strength and power of the Roman Empire, and an intimation of its ultimate demise [...] what the title does is signal the fact that in the end the internal contradictions of the empire finally were the seeds of its destruction ... while we don't see that happen, we know that this is where it goes, and that the slave revolt was one of the important elements in creating that historical fallout.[6]

This interpretation of the story is confirmed in the 'voice of history' prologue that opens the film. The message of the didactic opening is rather similar in style and content to the prologue of *Quo Vadis*—that Rome and its empire are always predestined to failure because the triumph of Christianity is inevitable, and that Christianity is a real spiritual liberation from the tyranny of Rome:

> In the last century before the birth of the new faith called Christianity which was destined to overthrow the pagan tyranny of Rome and bring about a new society, the Roman

Republic stood at the very centre of the civilised world . . . Even at the zenith of her pride and power, the Republic lay fatally stricken with the disease called human slavery. The age of the dictator was at hand, waiting in the shadows for the event to bring it forth. In that same century, in the conquered Greek province of Thrace, an illiterate slave woman added to her master's wealth by giving birth to a son whom she named Spartacus. A proud rebellious son, who was sold to living death in the mines of Libya, before his thirteenth birthday. There under whip and chain and sun he lived out his youth and his young manhood, dreaming the death of slavery 2000 years before it finally would die.[7]

This brief voice-over interweaves a conventional story of Rome's internal flaws and the eventual triumph of Christianity with the story of one heroic individual, and signals that *Spartacus* belongs generically in the same category as *Quo Vadis* and *Ben-Hur*.

The essential ingredients of this plot appear to be in keeping with *Ben-Hur*: Rome is cast as the oppressor, there is the potential for rebellion, there is corruption associated with excessive Roman power. Above all there is the promise of Christian salvation as the prospect of freedom from Roman oppression mentioned in the very first sentence. The prologue sets all this out, but there were some interesting conflicts to be resolved along the road to that beginning.

The original prologue: *not* the voice of history

Duncan Cooper's painstaking research has revealed the details of an earlier version of the film that begins on the eve of the final encounter with a pre-battle speech by Crassus.[8] This is not the conventional voice of history:

Nine Roman armies have been destroyed by Spartacus because they went out to fight slaves. Unless I am able to persuade you that the enemy we engage tomorrow is as formidable and skilful as any that you have met in your entire military career . . . then we too shall be defeated. And our defeat will mean the fall of Rome. The question is this: Why has a rabble of slaves been able to destroy the best troops the world ever saw? To answer that question you must understand that rabble. And most particularly, you must understand the man who commands them.[9]

The absence of a narrator at the start of such a film might indeed have been a bold gesture of departure from the genre's conventions. If Crassus' speech had been left at the start of the film, we might have had something much closer to a historian's way of looking at the events that are represented. The question Crassus asks and his suggested approach to answering it would set the film's story up as an investigation of a historical problem, and an exploration of a historical character, not just as a story of how power leads to corruption. Introducing the story via Crassus would also perhaps hint at the fact that the major historical source, Plutarch, does just that: Spartacus is a character in the *Life of Crassus*.[10]

Politically, this opening would have been far less open to the range of interpretations that are now applied to *Spartacus*, as has been shown by Maria Wyke and Martin Winkler.[11] Crassus' speech would have given us something more of screenwriter Dalton Trumbo's vision of Spartacus as a true revolutionary, and of his achievement as a real as opposed to imaginary or anticipated triumph of liberty.[12] Interestingly, Crassus' lines were used in a trailer for the film. This is a good example of how *Spartacus* advertises itself as something quite different from what it ultimately delivers; the battles Crassus refers to, although filmed as a montage sequence, were not actually included in the final film.[13]

There is yet another alternative beginning. It seems, from what Cooper says, that the prologue as we have it was rather hastily put together, and that the Christian message only came in at the very last minute to replace an even more defeatist but perhaps more historically minded version. In that earlier version, what strikes the most unusual note is the mention of historians:

> The historians of ancient Rome have recorded the death of his dream, and the utter destruction of his life and all his hopes. Yet his name still lives. And the last vestiges of slavery disappear before our eyes. And the defeat of Spartacus has become the victory of man.[14]

In the film we have now, historians' records get no mention, and the humanism of the earlier version is replaced with the destined triumph of Christianity. One has to presume that Maria Wyke is correct in surmising that Christianity was brought in to the prologue in order to create some coherence or balance with the closing scene and its religious overtones.[15] The previous version belongs to a more cerebral strand in the many developmental strata of the film. From the final version of the prologue it is hard to glean what story the film intends to tell, beyond the obvious one that power corrupts, and Rome is destined to fall because Christianity has a superior system of values.

The whip and the chain

Spartacus opens with a half-minute panning shot of a vast and arid mountainous desert landscape, through which long columns of slaves move, carrying heavy loads. The scene is watched over by only two Roman soldiers, positioned in opposite corners of the picture. In this case, the vastness of the wide screen is *not* a place for the display of masses of people or sumptuous sets but for the merciless travail of those pitiful creatures moving across it. The very width of the screen makes their tortuous labour seem all the more arduous. The whip and chain, it is clear from these images, are not intended as metaphors for tyranny as the 'whip and the sword' are in the prologue to *Quo Vadis*. This impression is confirmed by Anthony Mann's comments on the initial sequence (which he shot before Stanley Kubrick was hired): 'I figured the "message" would be conveyed better by showing *physically* the full horror of slavery. A film has to be visual'.[16]

These first minutes, before the introduction of Peter Ustinov's Batiatus, are a far cry from the 'synthetic Rome' condemned by the *New York Times* reviewer. The slaves are so covered in dust and dirt that they appear almost to blend into the landscape, and the relative absence of shiny red and gold Roman soldiers and standards gives the scene a very gritty and naturalistic look. The full horror of slave labour is conveyed at its most physical when, shortly after the end of the prologue, we see a man collapse under his load, the dry rock giving way under him as he begins to slide down the mountain. In the silent, physical drama that develops, Spartacus shows both his essential humanity, and the bestiality to which he has been reduced. In the midst of the horror of the labour camp, he attempts to help his fellow slave, is thrown to the ground himself and kicked like a dog by a soldier whom he then bites in the leg. Spartacus is punished by being chained to a rock where he will be left to starve—to set an example to others. At this point the screen is filled with the relentlessness of the slaves' suffering, while at the same time displaying the sheer power of Spartacus' body. He appears almost to become of a piece with the rock, a powerful image of his hardness and endurance.

I think that the film's unevenness begins with Batiatus' arrival. Ustinov is clearly enjoying this part, and appears to have taken great pleasure in the freedom to improvise and indeed rewrite his lines, effectively subverting the film's moral seriousness by refusing to take his own character seriously. It may be a great performance, but it can strike the wrong notes with its irony and self-consciousness, and at times creates incoherence in the film's narrative. For instance, in the opening scene Ustinov's knowing irony and the comic business with the slave and the parasol are simply not in keeping with Anthony Mann's visual set-up of a gruelling and relentless situation in a grim and inhospitable environment. Ustinov is too clever and comical, and too aware of the genre's clichés; he provides comic relief, which may be needed, but perhaps not quite so early, before the film has established its proper approach. Ustinov also steals the show rather, and begins to chip away at the centrality of Spartacus' character, although a brief and rather menacing close-up shot of Spartacus when his teeth are examined helps to remind the viewer whose side they are meant to be on, regardless of the entertainment provided by Batiatus.

Despite the intrusion of Ustinov, the opening scene sets a precedent, which Kubrick continues, of filming vast expanses of landscape (in California and in Spain) in which the slaves labour and travel and finally do battle. Ridley Scott may have had these memorable images in mind when he filmed Maximus' journey home to Spain and his transportation to Zuccabar in *Gladiator*. The antithesis between these landscapes and the Roman sets is exploited throughout the film, and it is clear that the landscapes are cinematically superior.[17] It is the landscapes that receive the real spectacular treatment, rather than any Roman reconstructions. Whether made for political or aesthetic reasons, that was perhaps a surprising choice: there is no evident historicity in the landscape, nothing about it that looks 'ancient'. Kubrick's (and Mann's) intention was to create a sense of the story of Spartacus as historical, but *not* in the manner of conventional epics. For this reason it may have been important to restrain the use of reconstructed sets and to embed the story in its natural environment instead.[18] Harsh and inhospitable landscapes were always a distinguishing feature of Anthony Mann's films.[19] This interest is shared by Kubrick, to whose films landscape is also frequently central, as can be seen in *Dr Strangelove* (1964), *2001: A Space Odyssey* (1968), or in *The Shining* (1980).[20]

Animals and Romans

After Spartacus is bought by Batiatus and travels to Capua the film exchanges the open landscape for the hostile and claustrophobic setting of the gladiator school, where it remains for the next forty minutes. During this time the theme of slavery that was introduced as relentless forced labour in hostile conditions in the opening scene becomes more complex. With Batiatus' speech comparing the trainee gladiators to pampered stallions ('Your bodies will be oiled'), it becomes clear that the gladiators are viewed as sexual objects, that there is an erotic dimension to the power wielded over them by the Romans. The sadistic training regime, the terrible voyeurism scene, the selection of the gladiators by the Roman women, the fight between Draba and Spartacus and the execution of Draba are all discussed by Ina Rae Hark in detail in the essay on *Spartacus* from which I borrow the title of this section.[21] Hark's argument is that together these scenes build up a picture of the gladiators as deprived of the very masculinity they must perform in the arena. All of this takes place in the film's first hour and thus appears to establish a strong thematic core.

During this hour it is striking that Spartacus himself hardly speaks, a silence imposed by Kubrick, who was persuaded of the importance of silence in films.[22] Spartacus says his name, in minute fifteen, and then a little later has a very brief and frustrating exchange with Draba, in which Draba's refusal to tell Spartacus *his* name introduces the apparent impossibility of friendship or society in the gladiatorial school. The theme re-emerges more urgently when Varinia, sent by Batiatus as a sexual favour, enters Spartacus' cell, and after a long silence he says, 'I've never had a woman'. One is reminded of the awfulness of the opening scene in the mines, the almost bestial existence that Spartacus led there. This extraordinary and much discussed scene, in which Batiatus and Marcellus are seen looking into Spartacus' cell (the camera captures them from below, from Spartacus' point of view) and taunting Spartacus to perform, concludes with his thrice-repeated outburst: 'I'm not an animal!' and Varinia's final response: 'Neither am I'.

Through this encounter with Varinia in the cell and their joint refusal to perform for the slave masters the foundation is laid for a story of Spartacus' humanisation, his journey from the silent savage who bites the guard in the first minute to the skilled orator and tactician of later scenes. For a further ten minutes, we see the gladiators training, and Spartacus looking at Varinia—still entirely silent, apart from asking her a question in the twenty-ninth minute.

It is not a fanciful interpretation, given this state of affairs, to say that the film's first act is about Spartacus' powerlessness expressed through the dynamics of 'the gaze'. The trainer and the dealer treat Spartacus as an object to be looked at for entertainment. Spartacus himself discovers that he is no object, no animal, and that he, too, enjoys looking—at Varinia. For him, this discovery brings with it the first recognition of his humanity. It becomes clear that the story this film tells of Rome revolves around two central themes: one is the difference between humanity and bestiality, the other is the Romans' perverted need to subject others to their gaze. In fact, Spartacus' first punishment, chained to a rock and starved to death—'to make an example of him' as the Roman commander puts it— emphasises a Roman obsession with displaying power and anticipates its apex: the crucifixion. Before the first twenty minutes of action are over, we have seen Spartacus branded like an animal, undergoing the quasi-sadistic spectacle of training at the camp, and covered in paintmarks by the trainer, who makes a mockery of Spartacus' gazing at Varinia, again intruding on the incipient relationship. In all, this exposition focuses entirely on Spartacus, on his suffering, and on the crucial issue of his objectification during this time.

The turning point comes when Draba refuses to cooperate with the Roman spectacular convention and throws his trident at the spectators. The sequence is famous for breaking the rules of transparent narration by aiming the trident directly at the camera, thus drawing viewers' attention to their own complicity. It also contains a shockingly violent moment, especially for the time it was made, when Crassus kills the already fatally wounded gladiator at his feet. In this sequence, beginning with the Roman women choosing 'their' gladiators and ending with Draba's breaking out of the prison of the arena, the power of those who are in a position to use others for their spectacular entertainment is thematised and examined very closely. The subversion of spectacle, when Draba refuses to follow the rules and dies for it precipitates the catastrophic events that follow. We see Draba's body suspended upside down from the ceiling— another spectacular example set to the other gladiators—and we begin to get a sense that they are ready to rebel. It jars a little that the rebellion itself only begins when Spartacus finds out the following morning that Varinia is being taken away. The realisation prompts him to speak (we are now in the fiftieth minute and the protagonist has not spoken since about minute twenty-nine) and then finally to erupt in violence against the trainer. Up to this point the strategy of linking Spartacus' rebelliousness to the humanity he discovers through falling in love with Varinia is not unintelligent—and is not just romantic fodder. Set against the arid loneliness and the quasi-bestial existence he leads in the desert where we first encounter him, Spartacus' meeting with Varinia is a powerful narrative tool.

Spartacus begins with a range of thoughtful and analytical approaches to the issue of slavery and its consequences, and indeed to the figure of the gladiator himself. Themes such as speech and silence, the possibility of community and the power of the spectacular promise a complex engagement with the ancient world. This connection resurfaces at the end of the film, although the middle is oddly off-target in its fixation with machinations in Rome.

Ending *Spartacus*: no view to a kill

The final third of the 189-minute restored version of *Spartacus* takes us from the failure of the escape at Brundisium to the final battle and the slaves' defeat, and concludes with Spartacus' crucifixion. A close reading of this 'third act' reveals much about how this film constructs both its plot and the worlds in which it takes place; it also shows how fraught the issue of the film's final vision really must have been. Like the opening, the ending was also subject to repeated and quite detailed revision—much of it clearly intended to water down any political or ideological inter-pretations in order to appeal to the widest possible audience.

The consequences for the film's dramatic impact as well as for its internal logic were quite serious.

Any potential success or superiority of the slave army appears to have been toned down almost out of existence, and replaced instead with a heavy emphasis on community and family. Visually, this emphasis is impressively brought out, for instance, in the golden, warm colours that suffuse a sequence in the slaves' camp, in complete contrast to the cold marble of the baths where the Romans discuss tactics. Great care has been taken to show, among the slaves, women, children, the elderly and deformed, and to place all this variety in a series of natural rather than architectural sets. Even this emphasis on the 'world' of the slaves in the film was not uncontroversial. Dalton Trumbo was dismayed when he found in a first cut that what he referred to as the 'world of the Romans' was drawn with far greater detail than that of the slaves in which, he felt, the film showed no real interest. At Trumbo's insistence, some of the crew returned to Spain and shot a great deal of additional footage of the slave camp. This is where the much-discussed emphasis on the familial, domestic aspects of the slave community—and the sense of there being a slave community at all—comes from.[23] As part of the story-telling, and of evoking the past on film, the advantage of this story about community is that it can be told just through images; no dialogue is necessary.

In terms of the film's politics, the battle montage and Crassus' speech about defeat by the slave army would have made this a very different story, one that did not fit at all with the conventions of historical epic in which the Roman sword is not overcome by other swords, but by spirituality. Trumbo had to settle for at least getting the film to show that the 'world of the slaves' was a powerful and valid counterpart to the 'world of the Romans'.[24] In this, once more, *Spartacus* is different from other films in the genre: the visual appeal of the slave scenes is not eclipsed by anything more impressive or memorable on the Roman side. Indeed, the Roman domestic interiors are decorative and artificial in a way that contrasts quite unfavourably in retrospect with the powerful realism of the location scenes.[25]

As the film nears its climax and end, Kubrick intercuts the two leaders' speeches before the battle in a very overt and self-conscious narrative technique that draws attention to editing and camerawork in order to highlight the differences between the two armies. Crassus is clad in heavy white and gold armour, surrounded by other senators and soldiers, and backed by the architectural detail of the Senate building. The uniform, social group and institution all symbolise Rome and ensure that we see Crassus as a representative of the city, not as a lone individual. Spartacus by contrast is filmed against the open sky, alone, and wearing his usual simple muddy-coloured tunic. He is addressing individuals whose faces are picked out of the crowd and focused on, their real commitment to their cause on display. Against this, we see that Crassus is addressing a faceless but orderly mass of soldiers all in identical armour, an inhuman war machine.

The battle itself is discussed below, but it is important to note how Kubrick shows the aftermath, especially the striking 'river of bodies' he created. Once more, the slaves are shown to be at one with nature as their bodies fill the valleys and are propped up against the hills: they *are* now the landscape.[26] Again, the camera movement is not transparent, instead it draws attention to the act of telling, or showing, the story—almost as though it were documenting it. The slow panning movement, focusing in extreme close-up on the bodies and on individual features intensifies the emphasis on community and family as the mass of bodies reveals couples, a father with children, hands stretched out to help one another. They may be defeated but Crassus, whom we appear to be following through this scene of devastation, is clearly uncomfortable in the face of the solidarity and brotherhood he witnesses. In an earlier version of the film Crassus had lines expressing his shock at the sight of the love between the fallen slaves and indicating the potential of this solidarity to triumph over Rome. The cutting of these lines is in keeping with Kubrick's conviction and it seems especially felicitous here as Olivier's silence at this point conveys more than words could.

The theme of solidarity and brotherhood continues to dominate the story with the famous 'I'm Spartacus' scene that sees the transformation of individual heroism into collective identity. This scene does have serious political potential; it also, to a degree at least, undermines the historical epic's preference for individual motivation over historical mass movements, precisely by dramatising how the personal can become political. Despite the strength of this scene, it is clear that the film continues to oscillate between different ideological positions as it moves towards its close.

Finishing things off: defeat or triumph?

A good example of the strange balancing act between defeat and triumph can be found in the exchange between Spartacus and Antoninus when they are captive and waiting for Crassus to arrive. The dialogue as we have it on the restored version from 1991 is this:

> *Antoninus:* Could we have won, Spartacus? Could we ever have won?
> *Spartacus:* Just by fighting them we won something. When even one man says 'No. I won't' Rome begins to fear. And we were tens of thousands who said it.[27]

In a widely distributed earlier version, Spartacus gives quite a different answer to Antoninus' question when he says, 'No. That was the wrong fight. We were doomed from the beginning. But it was a beautiful thing'.[28]

Doomed to failure, or a partial triumph against all the odds? I suspect that the film as we have it hedges its bets, and gives us a little bit of both, with the addition of the hope of ultimate salvation through Christianity as a kind of last-ditch attempt at conclusion. It is worth examining what exactly develops in the final minutes.

After the brief exchange between Spartacus and Antoninus we have a curious and perhaps not altogether cogent scene in which Crassus, frustrated with Spartacus' sullen non-cooperation, slaps him across the face with an anguished scream. Spartacus' response is to spit at him. Crassus' action is a final sign of his lack of moral fibre and lack of self-control. Having Crassus perform this weak, feminine gesture may be seen as a way of granting Spartacus the final moral victory. The Roman shows his enervated decadence, he is no match for the genuine masculinity of Spartacus. But the spitting unbalances things: it is not a particularly masculine gesture either, and returns Spartacus once more to the base creature who bit the guard at the start of the film, not the triumphantly redeemed and redeeming leader he had grown into through the film. It is unclear to me whether this is a deliberate decision, intended perhaps to show that Spartacus is morally and emotionally defeated, that there are no winners. We do know that Trumbo, who always argued for giving Spartacus more of a victory, was very unhappy with the spitting, which he found 'vulgar', and which clearly did not form part of his script.[29]

Perhaps the most striking and unsettling feature of this ending is that the two antagonists do not finally face each other in combat. Their only face-to-face meeting is the slapping-spitting exchange. Spitting and screaming aside, it is a courageous and innovative move to insist so radically on denying the viewer the conventional denouement associated with the Roman historical epic. In terms of the story the film tells, it is entirely consistent with Crassus' depraved and confused personality that he should think up an ingenious final way of torturing and humiliating his enemy and that he should avoid direct physical challenge. At this point, Crassus returns to his (and the film's) obsession with slave solidarity by announcing his intention to 'test this myth of slave brotherhood' by setting Spartacus to fight Antoninus. Depriving Spartacus of the chance to prove himself as a gladiator also means denying him the status of the conventional epic protagonist. Unlike *Ben-Hur*'s Judah, *Fall*'s Livius, and *Gladiator*'s Maximus, Spartacus is not given the opportunity of killing his enemy; the film thus cannot end even in partial triumph. Instead, the film consistently avoids and undercuts the spectacle of the arena, and this final fight is a mirror image of the first one between Draba and Spartacus, which was also a 'private show'. Now Crassus finally gets what he has wanted all along: the subjection and spectacle of Spartacus. Ina Rae Hark has written eloquently about this:

> By rigging the conditions of the fight so that to win is to lose, [Crassus] recuperates Draba's refusal to kill Spartacus by forcing Spartacus to kill Antoninus. Twice Spartacus has been part of a spectacle in which a slave resisted Rome's command to penetrate another slave against his or her will. Now he is trapped into following that script.[30]

For the purpose of Crassus' final subordination of Spartacus, an 'arena' is created by the soldiers who form a circle with their shields. It is worth noting here that both *Fall* and *Gladiator* reproduce this highly effective device. But around this arena there is darkness, and an absence of spectators to witness the spectacle. As in the earlier fight between Draba and Spartacus the absence of masses of spectators undercuts the gladiators' potential power; there is none of the glorification of the gladiator's persona through public adulation, no 'win the crowd' (as Ridley Scott's Proximo encourages Maximus). There is no crowd to win in this dark and lonely film. When Draba and Spartacus fight, one of the most distressing things is the relative lack of enthusiasm with which the Roman spectators are watching. In fact, the only instance of a gladiatorial fight performed for a cheering and enthusiastic crowd in the film occurs when the slaves make their Roman captives fight for them at Capua. They are severely chastised for their exuberance by Spartacus, who wants no part of this ('What are we becoming? Romans?' he shouts at them, as already noted above). Instead this final fight is closely observed by Crassus—a spectator whose immorality has been amply established by the narrative. It is filmed quite close up, and is also a relatively dark scene, so that what the viewer sees is high emotional drama between Antoninus and Spartacus. The ties between the two men, who view one another as father and son, are visually represented through the focus on their faces and through the choreography of the fight as, essentially, a long embrace. This scene is a most effective way of subverting viewers' expectations of the spectacular gladiatorial performance. The usual thrill of the Roman epic's arena scene in which the viewer can enjoy the visual excitement of the violent spectacle while condemning its immorality is not present here because the scene is visually obscure and morally complex.

What is substituted for the gladiatorial spectacle is not quite revolutionary brotherhood, but another instance of the film's emphasis on the domestic, familial aspect of the slave movement. The slaves are defeated into acting out their master's scenario, but within that scenario they are able, fatherless and childless as they are as slaves, to construct familial bonds. This is a form of triumph.[31]

Spartacus finally denies Crassus his victory when, cradling Antoninus' body, he utters the now famous line: 'He'll come back. He'll come back and he'll be millions'. The exchange between Crassus and Caesar as they ride away from the scene of Antoninus' death is intended to alert the viewer to the significance of the 'myth of Spartacus'. Crassus makes it clear that he is anxious for Spartacus not to become a martyr, a symbol of the revolution, when he asks for him to be crucified alongside thousands of others and not given a grave. The very final moments, in which Varinia shows Spartacus his son as Spartacus is dying on the cross, substantiate the sense that, though failed, the slaves' revolt reverberates in the future—and that it really was an important political undertaking.

The image of Spartacus crucified is not easy to read. Yes, there is a sense in which the crucifixion underlines his Christ-like status as a visionary who sacrifices himself for the future good of humanity (as hinted at in the prologue); this is supported, as many point out, by the visual reference to Mary made by Varinia's blue cloak and the baby in her arms. But it is also true that the long lines of crucified slaves that extend into the depth of the picture may undermine the Christian significance of crucifixion and alert us instead to the common use of this brutal practice in antiquity. In an alternative cut, widely circulated by 1967, we do not see Spartacus on the cross at all (only his feet, which Varinia embraces). Neither did Varinia's plea for his death and end to his suffering, or her promise to teach her son of his father's achievements and her assertion of the son's freedom appear in this version. As another attempt to finish with a very strong sense of defeat, this alternative ending is another example of how, as Cooper has shown, the film's political impact was under scrutiny for a long time. In the restored new edition by Ed Harris, what we have is, at the very least, potentially redemptive if not actually triumphant.

Still, this is an uneasy end, and it is not made easier by the final shot. This sees Varinia depart along the road lined with the crucified towards a future that may or may not be one of freedom, but which is forever marred by the presence at her side of the 'obese, craven, avaricious' slave-dealer and the two million sesterces he has been paid to deliver her to freedom.[32] This is bleak indeed. Kubrick himself appears to have felt ambivalent about the whole process of closure, as can be seen in this extract from his 'Notes on Film' published to coincide with the UK release of *Spartacus*:

> One thing that has always disturbed me a little is that the ending often introduces a false note .., When you deal with characters and a sense of life, most endings that appear to be endings are false, and possibly that is what disturbs the audience: they may sense the gratuitousness of the unhappy ending. On the other hand, if you end a story with somebody achieving his aim it always seems to me to have a kind of incompleteness about it, because that almost seems to be the beginning of another story.[33]

Revisiting *Spartacus*—2004

It is perhaps indicative of the unease over the end of *Spartacus* that a recent television film *Spartacus* (2004) has Varinia, after driving away on a cart (with a hired Roman escort, but *not* the slave-dealer) along the Appian Way lined with crucifixes, arriving and bringing up her son in a small rural community, a kind of utopian idyll—rather than Kubrick's 'indeterminate world where there exists only the certainty of death'.[34]

The television film revisits the whole dénouement of the Spartacus–Crassus–Antoninus triangle in rather an interesting way. Here, the Antoninus figure is the Jew David (resurrected from Howard Fast's novel that inspired the 1960 film and the 2004 version), who is captured and crucified by Crassus when the latter's attempts to find Spartacus are frustrated. But Crassus, as in Kubrick's *Spartacus*, is obsessed with obtaining Varinia's love. In the scene at his house, which is closely modelled in other ways on the earlier film, he eventually begs Varinia on his knees to love him. When she responds that he can never 'be Spartacus', he experiences an extraordinary vision in which he himself is about to be killed by Spartacus in the arena, while another version of himself leads the frenzied mob's shouts of 'Kill! Kill! Kill!' The gladiator-Crassus screams: 'I am Spartacus!' and his throat is slashed by the 'real' Spartacus. Immediately after this episode Crassus dismisses Varinia and goes to find David. Hanging on the cross, David continues to defy Crassus' pressure for information on Spartacus, and announces: 'I'll come back. I'll come back and I will be millions,' before Crassus in a rage plunges his sword into David's side. He is as impotent and frenzied as his cinematic predecessor, but also acting as a more explicit precursor of Christ's torturers in inflicting that particular wound on the crucified David.

On one level, all this is an ironic and knowing reflection on the earlier film, packing the two most famous quotes ('I am Spartacus' and 'He'll come back, and he will be millions') into a couple of minutes. But the dream sequence is also a cogent interpretation of the final fight between Spartacus and Antoninus: it is certainly the case that in a sense Crassus the voyeur uses

Spartacus as his stand-in, in the violence done to (the penetration of?) Antoninus, in the tenderness of the embrace and indeed in the kiss. The television *Spartacus* reduces the homosexual overtones, and so transfers Crassus' desire into a fantasy of violence, and links his desire to 'be Spartacus' to his heterosexual desire for Varinia. It also appears to make a quite overt connection between the slaves' fight for freedom and the rise of Christianity—surely that is the intended meaning of David's words on the cross. In this link with the promise of Christianity the 2004 version looks back to all those cinematic 'voice of history' prologues in which the 'whip and the sword' of Roman rule is defeated by the new religion. This would also make sense of the Roman senator Agrippa's closing statement in the series that seems to allude explicitly to the *Quo Vadis* prologue with the formulation 'the whip and the cross'.

Spectacle and Kubrick's Rome: the battle and the city

Spectacle, as we have seen, is what *Spartacus* is about, to begin with. The rejection of spectacle is what it ends with. But as a film set in the past, and a film of 'epic' length, which cost a lot of money to make, *Spartacus* is also expected to provide some displays of cinematic grandeur. These, I have argued above, are substantially found in filming of landscape, which exploits the potential of the Technirama system at its best. In this section, we will look briefly at two more aspects of spectacle in *Spartacus*. First, the battle between the slaves and Crassus' army; and second, the representation of the city of Rome.

The place where both Roman power and the power of cinema to recreate the past are displayed most spectacularly in *Spartacus* is the battle scene. For a twenty-first-century viewer, accustomed to scenes such as the opening of *Saving Private*

Ryan or *Gladiator*, the most striking thing about this sequence is how much of the battle can be seen at one time.[35] This scene exploits widescreen projection at its very best, creating a true panorama and filling the screen with extras and detailed action. The shots are quite long, allowing viewers time to take in the whole of the visual field and enhancing their sense of being 'on the balcony of history', as Roland Barthes put it when he first experienced CinemaScope. The relative lack of visible cutting and editing adds to the sense one has that what is shown on the screen is roughly what happened during filming; this adds to the sense of excitement about this kind of spectacle. André Bazin's condemnation of over-editing comes to mind: 'it is a question of respect for the spatial unity of an event at the moment when to split it up would change it from something real to something imaginary'. Arguably, what Kubrick presents with his battle is 'something real' or something that represents rhetorically, through its 'respect' for spatial unity, the idea of 'something real'. This may have consequences for how we think about such films as historiography. The battle in *Spartacus* could be seen to allow a distanced and critical view of the theatre of war, and of the violence perpetrated within it—frequently literally distanced by the fact that the camera affords a relatively wide angle. But it is also true that this kind of big shot is often motivated by the desire to display the lavishness of the production through showing off locations, sets, large numbers of extras, and so on. In drawing attention to the expense of the production, this kind of sequence is, in a sense, pure spectacle. The spectator's enjoyment in it may be tinged by the awareness of the similarities between our pleasure in this kind of spectacle, and the Romans' own desire for violent spectacles. The didacticism of the sequence (in showing the Roman formations as machine-like against the humanity and diversity of the slaves, or in lingering at some length over the bodies of the dead and wounded) is clearly an attempt to redress the balance for the spectator who has just been carried away with the thrill of the battle.

Kubrick's vision of the city of Rome is most prominently represented by a stark, almost modernist, and sparsely peopled Senate building. There is a brief initial panorama of the forum, which looks impressive in a conventional way and quite authentically crowded, but not overwhelming. This Rome is relatively unusual in cinema in that it is a republic, and so lacks an emperor or court. Crassus, decadent and self-indulgent as he is, endowed with a clearly dysfunctional sexuality as well as a somewhat pathological love of Rome, makes a very good stand-in for an emperor.[36] It is he who gives us a verbal description of the kind of spectacle that Rome usually offers in films when, after the famous 'oysters and snails' scene, he looks over Rome and makes of the city a symbol of power and eroticism:

> There, boy, is Rome—there is the might, majesty, the terror of Rome. There is the power that bestrides the known world like a colossus. No man can withstand Rome, no nation—how much less a boy? . . . There's only one way to deal with Rome, Antoninus: you must serve her, you must abase yourself before her, you must grovel at her feet, you must—love her.[37]

Perhaps the most striking thing about this speech—besides the masochism with which Crassus worships the city, and the sadism with which he wishes to dominate Antoninus in its place—is the fact that the film never visually portrays Rome in this way. Compared with some of the monumental sets of other films, and with the many allusions to European fascist regimes of other cinematic depictions of Rome, there is very little terror or might in Kubrick's Rome. Essentially, the glory and indeed the spectacle of Rome are in Crassus' mind.

There is one occasion when masses are gathered in the forum, which might qualify as the sort of epic spectacle we see elsewhere. But this occasion is Crassus' speech when he announces his attack on the slave army, and the scene is repeatedly intercut—and so explicitly contrasted—with Spartacus' own address to his people. Kubrick thus does not allow it to have the impact of the massive forum scenes in other Roman epics.[38] Elsewhere, a very interior and close-up Rome is contrasted with the vast open landscapes that the slaves travel through and camp in.[39] These journey sequences are panoramic, and they do represent a sort of historiography from the point of view of an omniscient narrator or protagonist, someone who has the clear overview allowed by the camera. But it is a significant aesthetic and political choice of the film that *Spartacus* reserves the panoramic epic perspective for the slaves rather than allowing it to represent the 'grandeur' of Rome in the way other films in this genre do.

The influence of Eisenstein's *Alexander Nevsky* (1938) claimed by Kubrick in the interview in 1960 quoted at the start of this chapter is not necessarily immediately apparent, but we have seen that it is true that the film departs in many ways from the established conventions of historical epic. Given how far it does go in its innovations of the genre, it is difficult to see how this uneven but interesting and often awkward film can be dismissed as 'heroic humbug—a vast, panoramic display of synthetic Rome and Romans, slaves and patricians, men and maids'.[40]

CHAPTER 4

THE FALL OF THE ROMAN EMPIRE
THE FILMMAKER AS HISTORIAN

I n an interview conducted with *Sight and Sound* after the 1964 release of *The Fall of the Roman Empire*, Anthony Mann identified one of the film's central problems:

> The problem with a set like that, of course, is that you have to fill it. Because of this it becomes a matter of mass movements instead of an individual movement; and the individual movement is more difficult to make in a huge set like that than a mass movement. It's fascinating to use masses but you don't always want to.[1]

For many audiences *Fall* was ultimately a failure because it provided no central protagonist that viewers could identify with and root for. However, as Martin Winkler demonstrates in his seminal essay on this film, it is precisely this absence of focus on a prominent individual that makes *Fall* so much more than just another cliché-ridden melodrama.[2] As Winkler points out, those who complain about the absence of a hero 'ignore the large canvas on which Mann must present and develop his theme'.[3] The use of the large canvas that puts to the fore history itself rather than a dominant individual is what makes *Fall*, according to Winkler, a complex and subtle piece of cinematic historiography rather than just another epic spectacle. As so often, the publicity machine tells a different story, in which *Fall* is very much placed in the tradition of grand spectacular epic—indeed it is advertised as the culmination of this tradition (see Fig. 3). Contrary to what the advertising declares, the approach to both story-telling and spectacle is indeed distinctive in this film. Mann's declared position was that 'the story is primary'.[4] He also stated (as did Wyler and Douglas before him) that spectacle was subordinate to character and story-telling:

> The story is told through the eyes of individuals rather than having chunks of spectacle and little characters in between. The first half of the picture is an intimate story of life and death and the characters bring you into the spectacle rather than it being imposed on you without any reason.[5]

Mann's approach to spectacle can indeed be quite idiosyncratic (the chariot race and the final duel between Livius and Commodus are frequently quoted as examples of this). The absence of a dominant hero encourages the viewer to examine the historical

3   *Poster for* The Fall of the Roman Empire.
Image from author's own collection.

events with more criticism than is usual in the genre. The emphasis on the role of groups or collectives (the fortress in Germany and its inhabitants, the assembled tribes, the army, the senate, the barbarian communities, and the Roman people in the forum) at the centre of the film is unusual and thought provoking. Above all, Mann's talent for filming overwhelming and vast landscapes and showing human struggle within those landscapes, demonstrated already in the opening scenes of *Spartacus*, contributes significantly to the story the film tells. The human figure never dominates the landscapes and must always appear as a tiny part of a much bigger context; this is probably the most serious historical point Mann's film makes.

Beginning: 'not an event, but a process'

As before, I will start by discussing the opening. *The Fall of the Roman Empire* has a lengthy credit sequence, with Dimitri Tiomkin's score launching into full orchestra after a rather portentous organ opening. The titles are displayed over what are meant to look like ancient Roman murals and graffiti, which are already discoloured and cracked. Arguably, antiquity is represented as material remains, as evidence for scrutiny, rather than as reconstruction. Not unlike the *Spartacus* title sequence (though without the stylish sparseness), this sequence announces the film as an intellectual endeavour, not mere spectacle. The weathered paintings also stand for the ruin of Rome, for its faded grandeur; the film thus announces from the start that it will contemplate the fall of a once great civilisation, 'musing amidst the ruins of the Capitol' as did Edward Gibbon, from whose famous historical work the title is borrowed. Mann is quite insistent on the historical validity of the film in a 1969 interview with *Screen*:

And for them to start to say 'This isn't Gibbon'—well this a lot of crap! . . . But you can't argue with these bums. They think they know it all. They said things weren't true. Well it was historically exactly true . . . These were all part of the things I had read. Then they scream and claim it's not historically accurate. It had more truth in it than untruth.[6]

The first shot, a long pan across a bleak and dark winter landscape in Spain is characterised by an absence of movement and activity, which is striking in contrast with the marching troops at the start of *Quo Vadis* and *Ben-Hur*, or the toiling slaves in *Spartacus*. Over this obscure and empty scene the prologue is delivered as the voice of the historian instead of the more conventional voice of history we have observed before. Written by the historian Will Durant, the author of *Caesar and Christ* (1944), the prologue sounds almost like a professor introducing a lecture on imperial Roman history:

Two of the greatest problems in history are how to account for the rise of Rome and for her fall. We may come nearer to understanding the truth if we remember that the fall of Rome, like her rise, had not one cause, but many. It was not an event, but a process spread over 300 years. Some nations have not lasted as long as Rome fell. In the year 180 AD the emperor Marcus Aurelius was leading his Roman legions against Germanic tribes along the Danube frontier.[7]

This opening is some way away from the triumphant beginnings of earlier films, not only in its insistence on tentatively approaching the 'truth' rather than proclaiming it, but also in the striking absence of any announcement of Christian salvation waiting in the wings to overturn Roman decadence. There are no obvious plot elements revealed here either, beyond the fact that Rome fell. It is rather a negative way of opening a story and the pessimism is confirmed by the first sentence spoken by the blind seer: 'My lord Caesar, the omens are bad—I could not find its heart'. The ensuing dialogue between Marcus Aurelius and his Greek adviser Timonides continues the sense of doom that dominated the voice-over. As though to deny the light of dawn that has now begun to illuminate the scene, the emperor continues to evoke images of nightfall and death: 'When I was a child, Timonides, I had a secret fear that night would come and would never end. That we would live out our lives in total darkness. It was a small fear then'. That total darkness and the image of Rome's long drawn-out fall will dominate the film—and make it less than engaging to some.

Whose story is it?

After the initial discussion between Marcus Aurelius and Timonides, the viewer has no sense of where the film is heading or who it is about. Livius arrives with (too) much fanfare during the film's fifth minute. Visually, his arrival does not do much to place him as the protagonist. The fortress and the forest dominate the picture, and Livius is obscured in full armour and helmet, riding in a chariot. Mann is extremely sparing in his use of close-up shots, preferring to give us a bigger picture. The viewer has to pick out the detail from the vast panorama. The relatively still and distant camera, and the prolonged shots can give an impression of detachment, allowing the viewer to act more independently in scanning the enormous screen for important detail. But overwhelming the protagonist with the landscape and the fortress also tells a very strong story at this point about the small place of the individual in the 'machinery of the Roman military empire' as Fenwick and Armytage-Green put it. For them, this first section of the film is the most successful as it accentuates 'the toughness at the heart of empire-building'.[8]

Livius' first lines are in a stilted conversation with Timonides regarding Caesar's health. A joke is then made by Marcus Aurelius at Timonides' expense, but it is very much over Livius' head. The emperor and the philosopher are completely in control of the story at this point and so far it is unclear what Livius' purpose will be. When he eventually moves into the centre of the screen, and we see him close up, his first words are: 'You are well, my Lord Caesar?' The camera now moves from him to Marcus Aurelius, where it spends most of its time during their exchange about events on the front.

When Lucilla is introduced, in close-up and praying, Livius can be seen in the right-hand corner, looking on. It seems that she has a mission—peace for the empire—but his narrative trajectory is still undetermined. When the camera closes in on him, he addresses Lucilla: 'Lucilla, you're beautiful'. The inanity of the remark, and perhaps its inappropriateness for an epic protagonist's first few words is not lost on Lucilla, who throws it back at him: '"You're beautiful"—what does *that* mean?' In the following exchange between them, she takes the initiative with the longer and more substantial speeches. So far, Livius is not doing too well as protagonist: he has had jokes made over his head, has admitted to failing to catch the leader of the German tribes, shown himself to lack understanding and knowledge of the emperor's strategy, and now he is being mocked by his beloved.

In the next scene, we get a notion of this film's story of Rome as more than a story of decay. Marcus Aurelius' *pax Romana* speech to the assembled barbarians offers a deeply optimistic vision of the empire as a 'family of equal nations'. The realisation of this ideal will form the film's narrative impetus and drive the action, even though it remains unfulfilled. Once again Marcus Aurelius and his alter ego Timonides are in the foreground as the camera switches between them and ignores Livius completely, until he once more comes up to the emperor to enquire about his health. Finally, twenty minutes into the film, Livius is charged with his mission: to succeed Marcus Aurelius and take Commodus' place. Even then, Marcus Aurelius announces this intention in conversation with his daughter; we only find after he has spoken to her that Livius has been standing in the room. At least we now have a hero with a mission. The seeds of a conflict are also sown as the differences between Commodus and Livius, and their established friendship, are outlined in the conversation between Livius and Marcus Aurelius. It is a further ten minutes before Livius speaks to Commodus and the two are established as antagonists. By contrast with the swift set-up of the conflict between Messala and Judah in *Ben-Hur* this is a very lengthy process.

A story of defeat

The antagonism between the two men is not central to the plot of *Fall* in the same way as that between Judah and Messala is in *Ben-Hur*, or Crassus and Spartacus in *Spartacus*. Instead we know from the prologue and from the action that develops in the first twenty minutes or so that the story is fundamentally an analysis of how the Roman Empire began to crumble. In terms of the three plot elements we identified as common to *Ben-Hur* and *Spartacus*, where does Mann's film stand? The first element— excessive power and the corruption that attends it—may be implied here. Marcus Aurelius' speech certainly shows that he is aware of this problem. The threat to the empire is perceived

to come from its edges and its borders and the emperor's vision
is about trying to avert its collapse. There is not, as in *Ben-Hur*
and *Spartacus*, an identifiable group of the oppressed seeking
freedom, but there is a sense that Roman power is becoming
permeable and difficult to maintain. There is no hint at a story
of salvation or conversion in *Fall:* the prologue deliberately and
intelligently omits any mention of Christianity, and there are
no explicit Christian messages to be found in the film to begin
with.[9]

Arguably, there are some parallels to be drawn between the
Christian salvation narrative of other films and Marcus Aurelius'
rejection of the principles of subjection and colonisation (and
implicitly slavery) that underlie Roman imperialism. His vision
of peaceful coexistence instead of oppressive Roman power may
have something in common with the ways in which in earlier
films Christianity is seen as the harbinger of freedom as well
as spiritual salvation. And when the senators in *Fall* later reject
Livius' proposal that the conquered Germans should be given
citizenship, the alternative to Marcus' vision of equality is spelled
out, and the implied connotations are made explicit: 'Crucify
their leaders, sell the rest as slaves'. Slavery and crucifixion, as in
Spartacus, *Ben-Hur* and *Quo Vadis*, are the tools of Roman power.
In his story, Mann only ever hints at the ways in which Christianity
may stand for freedom and for a better life. Timonides the Greek
philosopher shows himself to be a Christian by wearing the *chi-
rho* pendant, but this is the only explicit reference to Christianity
in the film. This helps convey the concept that the idealised little
community Timonides had created with the barbarians is both a
realisation of Marcus' ideas and an example of Christian society
in opposition to Rome's violence.

So overall Christianity and salvation do not play a role in *Fall*.
The film's dominant perspective is to look back to the reign of

Marcus Aurelius as representing a golden age in Roman history, and beyond that back to the virtue and simplicity of the republic.[10] This perspective owes much to an often-quoted sentence of Gibbon's *History of the Decline and Fall of the Roman Empire* (first published in 1776–78): 'If a man were called to fix the period in the history of the world, during which the condition of the human race was most happy and prosperous, he would without hesitation, name that which elapsed from the death of Domitian to the accession of Commodus'.[11]

This is not the sort of 'simple' or 'primitive' story Mann claims to favour. The situation gives the protagonist, and indeed the narrative itself, very little room for manoeuvre. Mann was well aware of this rather bleak pessimism, as he points out in the *Sight and Sound* interview: '*Fall of the Roman Empire* . . . has a defeatist theme. I was very conscious that I might be stepping into a hole in doing this because I just don't think people are interested in defeat'.[12]

The end: decline and fall

The final act of *Fall* starts when Livius and Lucilla are separated by Commodus and Lucilla is sent to Armenia. This takes place around two-thirds of the way through the film, at one hour fifty-five minutes. In a somewhat bewildering sequence of events, we see Livius dealing with a remaining troublesome tribe on the northern front, then being asked to confront a rebellion by commanders on the eastern front which turns out to have been initiated by Lucilla, and leads to a rift between the lovers. However, a surprise attack by the Persians (who are in collusion with the Armenian king) means that the Roman armies unite against them under Livius' command and defeat them. It is worth noting how little narrative excitement this battle generates, even though it is the only actual battle scene of the film, apart form the skirmish in the woods at the beginning. Even Winkler, *Fall*'s staunchest advocate, finds it 'uninvolving'. It is unclear to the spectator what exactly is at stake, who the opponents are, and what their motives are. The scene is shot in the style of a western, giving a good view of events from a distance, but it never gets off the ground properly mainly, perhaps, because of the lack of clarity over what the battle is *for*.[13] The Persians (who replace the historical but not popularly known Parthians for the purposes of the story) remain quite anonymous as opponents, and this increases the sense of detachment created by the distanced style of filming. As a piece of epic spectacle this really does not work. It could, however, be interpreted as an example of Mann's reliance on the interaction between man and landscape as a means of telling a story. Here Persians and Romans are both ultimately just human beings dwarfed by the landscape in which they toil for supremacy but which neither of them can ever fully dominate.

After the battle Livius declines Commodus' offer of co-rulership and the invitation to crucify and burn several thousand barbarians. As a part of this retribution Timonides' idyllic little settlement is devastated by Commodus' soldiers. Only thirty minutes from the end of the film Lucilla and Livius arrive at the scene and discover Timonides' body and find that the philosopher was a Christian. Now the distraught Livius is finally convinced that force alone will prevent Commodus destroying Rome. Nonetheless he prepares to give the emperor one final chance, and goes into Rome alone. At the feet of the statue of Jupiter Optimus Maximus he meets with a clearly deranged emperor, and subsequently with a senate that has also taken leave of its senses and turns against Livius when he tries to alert them to their responsibilities to the state.

This quick summary demonstrates the complexity of the story at this point—there are too many locations, too many different motivations, and too many different groups of people at play to make this a straightforward story. Added to this there is a relative absence of facial close-ups when compared with our other films so that the viewer's experience is more distant than is conventional in such a film. The story simply cannot be read as a story about a struggle between two individuals, or even between an individual and the state.

Finally Livius is led to the stake to be burned alive in the forum along with some of the Germans while the northern army is bought off with gold. Lucilla makes the decision to go into Rome herself and kill Commodus—we can infer this from the dagger she takes with her. There are now a mere twenty minutes left of the film and events follow swiftly upon one another. The city that she crosses in a chariot is now heaving with revellers, a huge tableau of total loss of responsibility, of complete decadence, and a splendid example of how Mann is able to fill the Roman set and let the masses of extras tell the story of the city's downfall.

Palace drama: how the set can tell the story

When Lucilla enters the palace intending to kill Commodus, and then asks Verulus, the gladiator who has been the emperor's constant companion, to commit the murder for her, it is revealed that Commodus is not in fact the son of Marcus Aurelius, but of Verulus himself. This, of course, paves the way for Commodus' eventual demise but it is a curious touch in this otherwise so 'objective' narrative. It personalises the story at this late stage with a retroactive reason for Commodus' clear unsuitability for office (as Verulus says: 'You should never have been Caesar'), as well as for Lucilla's difficult relationship with their mother that had been hinted at earlier. Commodus, already on the brink of insanity, now breaks down completely and kills Verulus.

The human drama of this scene is almost completely visually overpowered by the architectural set against which it is played out. Like the fortress at the opening of the film, this set now emphasises the insignificance of the human conflict when juxtaposed with the machinery or institution of empire that the imperial palace embodies. The revelation about Commodus' paternity, which Verulus makes to Lucilla, is filmed with the two interlocutors in close-up. Commodus has overheard, however, and we hear his anguished outcry 'It's a lie!' before he comes into the picture. He repeats the line twice as he enters from the right, but there is no close-up to show us his features, nor indeed his father's reaction to the denial. The two characters are separated by almost the entire expanse of the wide screen, which is dominated by the massive doorway with columns flanking it, elaborate arches along the ceiling and a heavily decorated floor. Verulus and Commodus move as on a stage. The enormous doorway continues to be at the centre of the shot for some time, even as Verulus attempts to convince Commodus of his paternity (his back turned to the camera) and Commodus continues to deny it (in profile, and half turned away from the camera). Commodus lunges at Verulus with his sword and is easily thrown back across the room. After this there is a very brief closer shot of Commodus as he begins to break down in tears. He turns away from the camera, which recedes almost immediately, allowing the spectator a view of Commodus' back as he approaches Verulus. Once more both are framed by the impressive doorway, and indeed a whole series of doorways that follow it in the depth of the set.[14] After the stabbing we follow the characters through these doorways, their backs turned to the camera until they reach the pool area, another splendid set that fills the screen while the actors remain on the right edge of the picture. Verulus falls into the water, and the camera never returns to Commodus but follows Lucilla's flight through the palace.

The sequence has been shot and edited with remarkable restraint so that it appears almost to be simply recording events. The absence of close-ups or any detailed reaction shots, for instance, means that there is not much overt narration going on. The viewer is left to understand events by observation from a distance, without much help from the camera as narrator. On the other hand, the gigantic set tells the story eloquently as it depicts the overpowering and ultimately weakening bombast and luxury of imperial life. Mann uses the palace set as he does his landscapes, to embed the protagonist in a battle with his environment. A tiny figure in the enormous palace, Commodus is an instance of one of Mann's trademark solitary figures battling against hostile landscapes. But in this case, the environment also represents the man—in its monumentality and ostentation it encapsulates the paranoid megalomania of the emperor.[15]

Another way of reading this scene would be to say that the almost total lack of engagement with the human face and body impoverishes it by making the simple acts of sympathy and comparison impossible. Part of what absorbs and enthrals film viewers is recognition of and identification with the projected human body. Without this the spectator can be left detached. Such alienation can, of course, be a positive outcome as it can increase an audience's critical appreciation of historical problems. It is a common technique of innovative and avant-garde drama and film, but in mainstream narrative cinema audiences expect to be able to engage more viscerally with events on the screen. Mann decides not to narrate the human drama of Commodus and Verulus using the kinds of techniques that would increase identification with the central characters. Instead he lets the viewer see this very intimate drama as part of a larger context in which human beings and their dysfunctional relationships are trapped in the grandeur and luxury of imperial Rome.

Ending: the voice of history returns

The real finale of the film is of course the fight to the death between Commodus and the condemned Livius. This takes place in the forum itself, where the Praetorian Guard create a sort of boxing ring (it is square rather than the round of the arena). This ring, completely shielded from the surrounding masses that we have just seen crowding the forum in celebration of their emperor, is where Commodus will now act out his fantasy of gladiatorial death. The guards and their shields entirely obstruct the view of the fight to those outside the ring. Instead, the camera adopts a bird's-eye perspective from a crane or some other elevation. This is intercut with shots taken from inside the enclosure. Both ways of filming draw attention to the camera as observer or narrator in a way that is not typical of unobtrusive narration. The view from above literally distances the spectator from the events on the screen even as it is skilfully contrasted with the closer angles from within. After a short while the perspective we share is that of the cynical observers on the steps above the ring, who begin to turn their thoughts to the auction of the vacant throne even while the two protagonists are still fighting for their lives. It becomes clear that Rome is no longer worth saving and that Livius is now only fighting for survival in order to be able to save Lucilla and the rest of the prisoners at the stake. The pointlessness of the fight is underlined by the fact that the people in the forum are quite oblivious to it, with the exception of those seeking to make money through it. The overwhelming pessimism that has characterised this film from the start and has effectively paralysed its protagonist comes to its close in this final scene—a fight to the death without a purpose. It is not surprising that this is the only one of our films that returns at its end to the 'voice of history' device.

Livius, of course, turns down the offer of the throne, and departs with Lucilla while the corrupt senators and military leaders haggle for the position between themselves. At least on the level of the individuals' story, there is a happy ending, even if it is only, as in *Ben-Hur* and *Spartacus*, away from Rome itself and its institutions. The final words, spoken over a magnificent panorama of the forum set, fires burning within, are those of the narrator: 'This was the beginning of the fall of the Roman Empire. A great civilisation is not conquered from without, until it has destroyed itself from within'.

We must conclude then, in agreement with Winkler, that history is 'the true "hero"' of Mann's film.[16] In Winkler's view, the absence of a central dominant and effective protagonist and thus the absence of the human motivation that is so crucial to classical Hollywood narratives is a positive influence. *Fall* certainly comes close to being a portrayal of history as a question, a debate, an interpretation. Like history, Mann's film is also obscure at times, with some *longeurs* and no strong sense of closure.

Spectacle and history: the triumph

When Commodus marches into Rome the smoke from Marcus Aurelius' funeral pyre dissolves to reveal the top of a triumphal arch against a very bright blue sky, and the camera sweeps down through the streets of Rome. Unlike his successor and imitator Ridley Scott, Mann does not film this scene in a flashy and coercive way, but rather uses his skill for filming landscape in the

magnificent set of the forum. As Fenwick and Armytage-Green
point out, Mann's technique is not to over-emphasise, but to let
landscapes speak for themselves: 'Rocks don't "frown", shadows
don't "loom", blue skies don't "mock". The scene is complete in
itself'.[17] In the triumph, the most openly spectacular sequence
of the film, Mann creates a panoramic but simple and realistic
point of view from which to follow the procession of gleaming
red and gold under a bright blue sky through the white marble
city. The set is, famously, by far the most authentic-looking
ever constructed,[18] and the path Commodus takes through the
forum and up to the temple of Jupiter Optimus Maximus on the
Capitoline also seems fairly accurate. Unlike the triumphs in *Ben-
Hur*, *Cleopatra*, *Quo Vadis*, or *Gladiator*, this does not take place
along huge plazas and boulevards that are more characteristic of
Mussolini's Rome or Haussmann's Paris but stays within a more
historical scale and layout. The skilful panning shots take in the
full scope and architectural detail of the set, lingering on a series
of vistas, all chosen to show off the set to the greatest advantage,
and it takes a full four minutes for Commodus to complete this
procession (compared with just over one minute for the 'same'
triumphal procession in *Gladiator*). But the relative lack of close-
ups—for instance of faces in the crowd, or of the protagonist
himself—and the static point of view of observation from outside
contribute to make this scene, like the battle, difficult to engage
with emotionally. In *Ben-Hur* we were able to see the triumph
through Judah's critical eyes and so had an individual to identify
with in the masses of people moving across the screen. Mann's
perspective appears more objective. His aim is to show what a
triumph was like and he achieves this rather splendidly. What
viewers may want, though, is to get a feeling for what it was like
to be present at such an occasion. That is where Mann's admirably
detached perspective fails to deliver. In the balance between

story and spectacle the viewer is temporarily overwhelmed by spectacle since the protagonist who ought to be providing the point of view (as Mann himself asserted) is absent.

Spectacle and history: revels in the forum

Near the end of the film there is perhaps a better example of how individual experience and massive spectacle can be integrated to tell the story. When Lucilla flees the palace after Commodus' murder of his real father she emerges onto the streets of Rome, which are now heaving with the celebrating masses. The camera follows her closely as she cuts her path through a sea of revellers, and here Mann has realised extremely successfully the image of the individual caught up in the sweep of history. The scene contains both long shots of the Roman forum and the masses and close-ups showing the protagonist's distress. Lucilla is seen pursuing her individual aim of reunion with her lover, and the conflict between that personal interest and the sweep of the historical event (in this case, the complete undoing of Roman civilisation) is powerfully evident.

A good comparison is a similar, though perhaps even more successful, sequence from *Gone with the Wind* (1939), the great American civil war epic. In this sequence, discussed in detail by Pierre Sorlin in his important book *The Film in History* (1980), the protagonist Scarlett O'Hara is trying to find a doctor in the chaos of a makeshift military hospital in the besieged Atlanta. What is striking and memorable about the sequence is its combination of historiography with the focus on the individual narrative and character that make it good cinema. This is largely a result of the restraint shown by the director in the display of the expensive set and extras. Rather than start with the long panning perspectives that would make the most of the huge expanse of wounded bodies, the sequence initially focuses exclusively on Scarlett and on her point of view. As Sorlin has pointed out, one of the most effective aspects of the scene's editing is that the spectator, with Scarlett, is made to ignore the wounded and dying during her desperate search for the doctor.[19] When the camera eventually slowly moves away from Scarlett, and a bird's-eye view shows us the extent of the chaos surrounding her, it becomes clear to the spectator that there is no chance of individual salvation in the face of historical events. The important thing about the scene in *Gone with the Wind* is that Scarlett at no point shows any awareness of the larger import of the events around her. She is only an individual trying to survive the overwhelming tide of history. Her unawareness heightens the irony of the scene, and it makes the viewer more alert to the significance of the events without any need for words to spell this out. By contrast, Mann has Sophia Loren as Lucilla intone an internal monologue as she moves through the crowds. In turning her into a kind of histori-cal prophet the script loses sight of the intimate story between Lucilla and Livius. I suspect that the aim of the scene was to inte-grate the character into the historical narrative and to show that individual suffering and historical decay are linked. In fact, the images on the screen were eloquent enough on their own to tell the story of the utter corruption that has taken hold of Rome; Mann himself has stated repeatedly how important it is in film not to let words overshadow images. Lucilla's anguish at being separated from Livius by the dreadful turn of events needed no words to express it, but perhaps Mann really did see her first and foremost as a voice through which to comment on the historical events. That is certainly what he implies in the *Screen* interview when he says that 'she feels it and sees what is happening in the world and tries to scream it out'.[20] He concludes by telling the interviewers that 'it took a lot of guts to do it this way', which may suggest that he is aware of the potential pitfalls of the voiced internal monologue.

After the lovers are reunited at the stake, the camera does not stay with them or with the individual story but once more pans out to show the crowds in the forum. Now we have a fine example of how Mann can let images speak for themselves. The tragic story of Rome's fall is eloquently told by contrasting the fine architectural detail (by filming through the monumental arch, with the victory columns running down the centre of the screen) with the pathetic loss of control exhibited by the crowds. No words are necessary to express that the frenzied revellers are not worthy inhabitants of the beautiful city. In this Roman forum there should be political debate and rhetorical excellence to mirror the cultural achievement displayed by the lovingly reconstructed buildings.

In all, it seems clear that *Fall* has to be looked at very seriously. Certainly, there are fine examples of what cinematic historiography can achieve in the first half of the film, with the use made of the forum set and the imperial palace to tell compelling stories about the fate of Rome and of the individuals caught up in its crumbling institutions. It seems perverse that the *New York Times* critic Bosley Crowther should recognise the value of *Ben-Hur*, even defend *Cleopatra* against sustained criticism, but condemn *Fall* as lacking in human interest and label it a 'murky accumulation of Hollywooden heroics and history'.[21]

CHAPTER 5

GLADIATOR
MAKING IT NEW?

R idley Scott's background in advertising did a great deal to help reinvigorate the tired epic genre. It is fair to say that much of the excitement over *Gladiator* in 2000 was a result of its success in making historical epic look sexy and modern. It may seem odd to start with observations about the production design until one realises that Scott himself does the same thing. As he said to an interviewer for *American Cinematographer*: 'When I'm in prep on a period film, the people I probably do the most work with are those in the art department'.[1] In the same interview Scott asserts how important it was to bring a different look to antiquity and that this was achieved through the production design. There are some prominent visual characteristics that exemplify *Gladiator*'s modernity. First, like many contemporary films, it consistently prioritises close-ups over wide-angle perspectives, so that it rarely appears to be a staged historical tableau. In close-up, the characters' historicity is less important than their humanity—they could be anywhere, anytime.[2] Second, the film's fast cutting and the use of steadicam in particular, which are ubiquitous in contemporary films, mean that *Gladiator* can be viewed as a contemporary action or adventure film rather than necessarily being categorised as 'epic' in the mould of the 1950s or 1960s. Third, the costume design frequently departs from conventions (for instance, lengthening the men's skirts enough to cover their knees, bordering senators' togas in black rather than purple) in order to avoid a clichéd 'period' look. Aesthetically *Gladiator* is a departure from some of the generic conventions of Roman epic movies. Does it tell a new story, too? Is it indeed a film about Rome at all, or merely, as one critic puts it, 'a wallowing in the Roman look'?[3] Is there more to *Gladiator* than the spectacles of violence in the Colosseum for which it is chiefly known? Does it achieve the famous balance between story and spectacle that each of our films so far has sought to deliver? Some say that through its subtle negotiation of the tension between narrative and spectacle *Gladiator* delivers an implicit critique of the spectacle it produces with such efficacy.[4] In this chapter we will attempt to unravel how and if this might be true.

Beginning: up close and personal

Like many recent films, *Gladiator* has no opening credits sequence beyond the production companies' logos and the title of the film. There are therefore no images of statues or paintings, or anything to signal that the film is set in antiquity. Instead of the voice of history that was popular in the 1950s and 1960s, the film opens with a rather sparse written prologue over a background of a sepia sky. The music at this point is restrained, spotlighting Lisa Gerrard's very effective, vaguely eastern-sounding vocals. In the course of the film Hans Zimmer develops a full-scale, frequently Wagnerian, orchestral and synthesised extravaganza, but Gerrard's motif is reserved for Maximus throughout and thus ensures that the viewer is aware of his estrangement from his surroundings.[5] At the start of the film the 'Elysium' theme, introduced with a shot of a field of wheat, ensures that the film

opens with the emphasis on the protagonist's 'inner journey',
as it means to proceed. It might appear that the film's opening
minimises the overt signs of narration that we have come to
associate with historical film, yet some familiar motives have
crept into the brief prologue text—as though to alert the viewer
to the film's status in a series of such films:

> At the height of its power, the Roman Empire was vast,
> stretching from the deserts of Africa to the borders
> of northern England. Over one quarter of the world's
> population lived and died under the rule of the Caesars.
>
> In the winter of 180 AD, Emperor Marcus Aurelius'
> twelve-year campaign against the barbarian tribes
> in Germania was drawing to an end. Just one final
> stronghold stands in the way of victory and the promise
> of peace throughout the empire.[6]

As in previous film prologues, the emphasis is on Rome's
size, power, and domination of others. One might compare,
for instance, 'centre of the Empire and undisputed master of
the world' in *Quo Vadis*, with 'had lain under the mastery of
Rome' in *Ben-Hur*, and 'at the zenith of her pride and power' in
Spartacus. But, on the face of it, this prologue paints a picture of
the empire as benign as well as powerful. There is no mention of
the rise of Christianity or of Rome's weakness or fall. Of course,
many twenty-first-century viewers will be suspicious of the very
mention of the words 'victory' and 'empire'; and I suspect that
it is possible to see in the phrase 'at the height of its power' an
allusion to the idea of a fall (from that height).[7] It is possible also
to see the idea of people 'living and dying under the rule of the
Caesars' as a hint at the enslavement of those people, and as a
hint at the totalitarian aspects of such a system. However, obvious
hindsight and the anticipation of Christianity, both of which are

common to the other prologues we have looked at, are avoided. In its simplicity and lack of didacticism this prologue does not seek to establish generic continuity in the way that earlier films do.

Scott does not start with Roman legions moving through the landscape or with Roman roads or slaves. The opening shot is a long close-up of a hand stroking the golden wheat in a field as its owner walks through a field. This image initially appears to have no narrative significance, but is soon understood as a synecdoche for the protagonist's home and farm—and later for death and the afterlife. The image of the hand, followed by Maximus' head and shoulders dominating the screen immediately afterwards, achieves a complete focus on the protagonist. He is not clearly understood as a Roman soldier at first, although he looks vaguely military, and clearly not modern. All that can be seen of his costume at this point is a bit of breastplate and some fur draped over the shoulders. He wears no plumed helmet and we cannot see his legs so that there is no skirt to give him the appearance of a Roman soldier in the cinematic tradition. All this contributes to making Maximus less visibly a historical figure. The absence of overt costuming at this point helps viewers to see him as someone they can identify with. He occupies the screen alone for the first couple of minutes of the film, and the viewer gets some idea of the other, non-military side to his character in the brief contemplation of the rather charming robin on a branch. It is clear that Scott wants to begin his film in this way precisely to avoid the look of the historical film; but he also signals very clearly with this opening that he may be more interested in the isolated individual Maximus than he is in the bigger historical picture.[8] In two-and-a-half minutes these images have told a complete story: this is a military man who prefers the simple life of the country and who seeks solace in contemplating nature. He has a tender heart underneath his tough exterior.

Now that we know whose side we are on, the story can turn to the battlefield. In a cold, dark, bluish dawn, very like that at the start of *The Fall of the Roman Empire*—from which Scott has borrowed heavily—a more familiar historical scene is developed, with troops traversing the field. But Scott is keen to stay with his protagonist and with the focus on individuals as he prepares the spectacular battle sequence. Visually one of the most striking differences between this opening of *Gladiator* and, say, that of *Spartacus*, is the extent to which the camera lingers, close up, on human features—not just the protagonist's but those of a whole range of extras. One result of this emphasis on faces is to distract from the feel of 'period drama' by picking out individuals rather than showing a historical feature known as 'the Roman army'. But this is, as we discussed in the first chapter, a form of story-telling: the camera guides our gaze to see the faces of the soldiers, their loyalty to Maximus, their exhaustion, and so on. All of it is building up Maximus' story for us.

The chopped-up, often mumbled dialogue at the beginning creates the sort of slight disorientation one often experiences in the opening minutes of American thrillers: it is about scene and atmosphere rather than conveying information or reflection. Maximus' first words, referring to the troops, are 'Lean and hungry'. It is a fragment rather than a speech, and focuses on action, not especially historical or ominous. The brevity of his few initial remarks also helps to establish Maximus' dominance as, for instance, when he overrules the judgement of his right-hand man Quintus swiftly and assertively ('Range is good'). In the same laconic, markedly *modern* way the issue of Rome as conqueror, familiar from the prologues of earlier films, is now introduced. Quintus, observing the Germans' insistent and savage, though doomed, resistance, says to Maximus that 'People should know when they're conquered'. Maximus now tries on the position of the rebel he will soon become, when he replies: 'Would you, Quintus? Would I?'

'Let me go home': a character's journey

It has been noted elsewhere how close the opening battle is to the groundbreaking opening scene in *Saving Private Ryan*.[9] The allusion helps to establish the film in a context other than that of the historical epics of the past. In the battle Scott avoids the visual clichés we associate with historical epic and uses instead some of the formulas of the modern war film (gory close-ups, extreme sound effects, hand-held cameras, very heavy, chopped-up editing, and some slow motion) to create a very effective scene. Throughout almost the whole of this Maximus is on the screen; in the film's tenth minute he is on the ground, his face bloody, narrowly escaping being hacked to pieces by Germans. Twelve minutes into the film, the battle is over already and Maximus proclaims victory. Now the camera closes in on the watching emperor, and on his evident despair at the brutality he has just witnessed. Through Marcus Aurelius' eyes the spectacle of violence is criticised and the viewer reminded of the correct point of view—but only after Maximus' victory has been enjoyed. This perspective is reinforced very shortly afterwards by Maximus' response to inspecting the hospital tent where the wounded are treated after the battle. As he washes his bloodied hands in close-up it is clear to the viewer that the human cost of the gory spectacle is central to the story the film will tell. In this way story and spectacle can be seen to balance one another: spectacle gives viewers what they want to see in the cinema; the story-telling justifies it or reflects on it and embeds it in the narrative.

Before fifteen minutes have passed, it becomes clearer still that neither emperor nor general are keen on any more battles and Maximus has asked for his reward: 'Let me go home'. Commodus is established as the antagonist, excluded from the relationship of understanding between Maximus and Marcus Aurelius. This becomes especially clear when Marcus in an ironic and conspiratorial tone remarks to Maximus (while Commodus looks on, excluded): 'So much for the glory of Rome'.

Commodus, on the other hand, appears to believe in the glory of Rome. He is more obviously a classic Hollywood Roman, with his talk of games and sacrifices. He also looks more like a character in a Roman epic film, swathed in gorgeous furs and fabrics and surrounded by the trappings of what we recognise as 'Roman decadence'. His first scene sets up his ambition to rule, his 'scheming' (referred to by Lucilla), and the potentially unhealthy feelings he has for his sister. All this is of course part of the repertoire of the 'bad emperor', both in ancient history and in the movies. It helps to set up, very swiftly, the opposition between Commodus and Maximus that will become the film's backbone. The secondary opposition, the political question of 'republic or empire', is also set up within the first twenty minutes, when Maximus' brief and reluctant exchange with Commodus and the senators introduces the potential of political intrigue and corruption. This gives Scott the chance to establish more firmly still Maximus' position as outsider. When asked if he aims for Rome now, his answer is unambiguous: 'Home, my wife, my son, the harvest'.

These initial images have very rapidly established a story in which Rome is an efficient conqueror of savage rebels and ruled by a philosopher-king who provides a complex perspective on the wisdom of such conquest. The reluctant but brave and honourable general—a clear 'outsider' similar to Mel Gibson's character in *The Patriot* (2000)—is surrounded by the beginnings of intrigue and politics, and antagonised by an archetypal, dysfunctional and morally corrupt Roman 'insider'. It is clear from this early point that what Maximus strives for (and therefore what the narrative aims for) is the return home, and not any military or political goal.

Substantially, *Gladiator* is the story of its protagonist, but does it also succeed in telling a story about Rome, and is that story new or different? As in our other examples, we are looking at a Rome characterised above all by military strength and the subjection of others. The set-up hints at the fact that this is problematic but not by forming a retrospective judgement through the eyes of history. Instead, the judgement is delivered from within, through Marcus Aurelius and through the figure of Maximus himself as the reluctant leader. The idea of absolute power that corrupts is delivered in a more conventional manner through the character of Commodus, emblematic of the 'bad Romans' in the mould of Crassus in *Spartacus*, or *Ben-Hur*'s Messala—and of course *Fall*'s own maniacal Commodus. The notion of an oppressed group or individual who might rebel or rise is introduced in the Germanic tribe's insistent insurgence, and is planted firmly in our minds through Maximus' hint of empathy with them at the start of the film. But, in keeping with the conventions of the modern action cinema, insurgence in *Gladiator* becomes a matter of a lone individual's struggle against an oppressive or authoritarian establishment. Rome is a machine of war and repression that Maximus has served faithfully, and which he now longs to escape. The plot will develop along the line of this tension that sets Rome against home.

This can be seen as a modern and perhaps simplified version of the opposition between Romans and Christians/Jews/slaves. As others have shown, the groups that oppose Rome in the traditional epic films are almost always characterised by good, functional, family units and strong domestic environments: the very things the Romans are unable to achieve. The protagonist in *Gladiator* is distinguished by his association with a family unit and by his commitment to home and fatherhood. Unlike Spartacus, though, Maximus does not obviously stand for a particular group. His political commitment to the republic, as we are reminded repeatedly throughout the film, is only secondary to his commitment to his family. His true goal is not to lead Rome towards a better future, but to leave it behind for the sake of private fulfilment, even if that can only be found in death.

Finally, I suggested earlier that most cinematic stories of Rome have in common a narrative of implied or actual conversion as the only feasible solution to the doom of Rome. In *Gladiator* there is no Christian plot, and yet salvation is at the core of the story it tells. This is achieved mainly through the film's guiding motif of the after-life, introduced in Maximus' first speech and reiterated throughout the film. His embrace of that after-life is Maximus' enlightenment—and his own salvation. The 'emotional journey' of its hero, as the producer Walter Parkes puts it, is at the core of *Gladiator*, and it is what ultimately assured its commercial success.[10] Indeed, Maximus' spirituality is given a prominent airing around thirty minutes into the film when we see him praying to a set of anthropomorphic figurines, whom he addresses as mother and father.[11] The praying is offset by a brief memory sequence that introduces the characters of Maximus' wife and son. The point of this scene is to establish Maximus' spirituality as private, linked to his family, and separate from the worship of well-known Roman deities or the performance of sacrifices that might be typically associated with Roman beliefs. This is in contrast with Commodus' ostentatious and conventionally pagan religiosity, as demonstrated in his announced intention to 'sacrifice a hundred bulls' after the battle. Marcus Aurelius, whom we are encouraged to see as a sceptic vis-à-vis Roman religion, perhaps because of his stoicism, asks Commodus to 'save the bulls'. While Maximus' ancestor worship is evidently meant to evoke the idea of the Roman *lares*, one cannot help but suspect that his prayers are also intended to introduce a very modern kind of spirituality, more private than institutional, at the core of which is a notion of the stable family unit. In this way, Maximus is distanced from the more alien world of pagan Rome and its rituals and brought closer to the modern world.

The right ending

The production of *Gladiator* did not start with a particularly clear idea of the story the film was going to tell. What was plain was that this was to be a film set substantially in the Colosseum, and that the protagonist was to be a gladiator—that was the rather minimal pitch that was sold to Steven Spielberg by the producers and by the original writer David Franzoni, who came up with the idea.[12] After this, as is often the case in contemporary Hollywood productions, the script went through a long series of changes and rewrites. The set-up, which we have just examined, was the only firm point when production began. It is interesting to see how hard the film has to try towards the end to come round to 'the right ending'.[13] For instance, Maximus' perfect death and release in the arena may in fact be a pragmatic response to the financial problems associated with the preferred ending, which would have seen Maximus enter Rome with 5,000 troops and putting an end to Commodus' tyranny.[14] That ending is what we are originally led to expect when the final act begins after Maximus' successful defeat of Tigris.

Despite Commodus' attempts to gain the upper hand ('You simply won't die' and the horrible taunting with the suffering of the wife and child), Maximus is now entirely in control of the situation, and will remain so for this final act, during which he no longer behaves as an entertainer but a general. Immediately after this confrontation with the emperor, Maximus catches sight of his servant Cicero, to whom he asserts his status and determination: 'Tell the men their general lives'. Maximus initiates a meeting with Lucilla and her accomplice, the senator Gracchus, and informs them how he will liberate Rome and kill Commodus. In order to emphasise this new phase in the character's journey, we see Maximus during this meeting with a blanket draped over his shoulders to give him (as Russell Crowe says on the commentary) a more 'regal' air, instead of the old tunic he has worn so far.

The plan is foiled by the emperor's informers, but not before the very real danger posed by Commodus to Lucilla and her son has been established. The story is intent in this last act on making events personal not political. We are given the strongest taste yet of Commodus' incestuous desire for Lucilla. The romantic link between Lucilla and Maximus is finally established now: the kiss between them counteracts Commodus' conflicted attempt at kissing her just before. In this way the narrative overlooks the political plot in favour of a very strongly personal story as the film reaches its end. Commodus' famous 'busy little bee' scene, in which he casts himself as the emperor Claudius, is a good example of the self-reference and irony the film likes to indulge in from time to time, especially through the person of Commodus. That scene forms the endpoint of this act, and seems to seal the fate of Lucilla and Lucius. They are caught in a plot from Robert Graves' *I, Claudius*, in which intrigue and politics always have the upper hand. It seems unlikely now that their action-film hero is going to be able to help them.

With twenty-three minutes to go (in the 2005 extended version), Maximus has been betrayed by Lucilla in order to save her son, and dawn is rising over a panorama of Rome seen from the emperor's palace. Commodus appears in front of this view, his darkness dominating the golden tones of the vista of Rome behind him. He is the demon who is now in total control of the dream and the light that was Rome. As he makes his claim on Lucilla and her son the camera moves away from the window with him into the interior of the room—*this* is Rome now, the drama of a dysfunctional family within a room dark with shadows.

At this point, the fourth and final part of the film begins as we find ourselves back in the arena. Listening to the crowds cheering for Maximus above them in the Colosseum, the emperor faces Maximus, who is displayed not unlike a crucified man, with both arms chained above his shoulders, and with crossed beams just hinting at a cross behind him (given Scott's keen eye for such detail, this image cannot be accidental). In another self-referential turn, Commodus echoes the film's advertising slogan and alerts us to our own position as spectators: 'They call for you. The general who became a slave. The slave who became a gladiator. The gladiator who defied an emperor. A striking story. Now the people want to know how the story ends'.

Several layers of the story are completed after this. First, in a nice bit of ring-composition, Commodus stabs Maximus in an embrace mirroring the murder of his father and reminding us of the political aspect of Maximus' journey, and of the battle for succession and for the establishment of proper father-son relations. The dying Maximus then enters the arena for one last big spectacle alongside Commodus; for one last time the 'mob' is to get what it deserves. One last time, too, *Fall* provides a foil for what we see here. But where Mann creates a deliberately obscure and anti-spectacular sequence, Scott puts everything into this finale. Built into this final thrill is the theme of Maximus' homecoming in death, as he repeatedly reaches for the home he now sees before him in the images of 'Elysium' and home that flash before him.

His personal journey is over now, but he still has a political function to fulfil, and Maximus aims to do his duty by Rome, even as he is dying. To this end, he gives orders to Quintus regarding the prisoners, and announces that the 'dream that was Rome' must be realised according to the wishes of Marcus Aurelius. The vagueness of this command is of course entirely in keeping with the film's indeterminate politics overall, and it ensures that any political messages remain at best implicit (at their worst they are incoherent). We return to the field we remember from the opening scene, and with Lisa Gerrard's vocals rising once more, our hero crashes to the ground. The film ends with Maximus' return to his wife and son in the after-life—a hero's homecoming, and the retreat into private life he has been striving for throughout. More than that, perhaps, this ending asserts the triumph of fatherhood, of a certain kind of unambiguous and domesticated masculine authority, as Maximus breathes his last words to Lucilla, 'Lucius is safe'. The 'dream that was Rome' turns out to be after all, as William Fitzgerald has put it, 'the name for the unrequited desire for an authority that would restore the public world to these anachronistic men'.[15]

'Now we are free'

The ending really belongs to Juba, the African gladiator who has been Maximus' companion since the beginning. We see him burying the quasi-*lares* that Maximus has been praying to, uttering the words 'Now we are free' as he does so. Once again, what we have here is a curious mixture of the personal and spiritual with the political. It is clear that on one level the image of the black African slave speaking of freedom is making a political point, albeit a new one to this film, which has not bothered overly with the politics of slavery before this moment. In fact, I suspect that what political impact this moment has is 'extra-filmic', in that it has more to do with the actor Djimon Hounsou's public image, achieved primarily through his role as the leader of the slave rebellion in *Amistad* (1997).[16] Through that earlier role as a kind of African Spartacus, and through the allusion to the relationship between Draba and Spartacus in Kubrick's *Spartacus*, an anti-slavery message does creep into the picture. However, Peter Rose is right in asserting that Juba is substantially subordinate and unquestioning towards Maximus, and that the politics of this is entirely contrary to the politics of Hounsou's role in *Amistad*.[17]

Juba's scene offers no more than a hint at the political struggles that are central to both *Spartacus* and *Amistad*. The burying of the figurines, which have somehow become associated in the viewer's mind with Maximus' wife and child, even if this has not been made explicit, overlays what political message there is in Hounsou's utterance with the insistence on the centrality of the family to the film's story. What then are the film's final messages? That Maximus' sacrifice has brought freedom to Rome and to his African friend. That his faith in the little ancestor figures paid off, and that family is the most important value in life. That salvation therefore is to be gained from and in private life. Scott cannot resist one last grand gesture. The final shot takes us from a darkened and abandoned Colosseum (will there be no more games in the new era?) into a panoramic view of Rome as seen from the top of the Colosseum, a new dawn rising over it. Looking more sumptuous than ever—and more than ever like a nineteenth-century painting—and combining urban and pastoral visions of Rome, this image conveys the notion (however absurd) that the city has been returned to a new golden age.

This, we are clearly meant to understand, is 'the dream that was Rome'.[18]

Creating worlds: Rome as spectacle

Scott's first view of Rome is a glamorised version of Hitler's arrival at the Nuremberg rally from Leni Riefenstahl's propaganda film *Triumph of the Will* (1935).[19] Of course, Scott's intention is to convey the sinister aspects of Commodus' Rome, which he casts as a totalitarian regime in direct opposition to the dream of the republican Rome that it is Maximus' task to restore. We are meant to see Commodus as the oppressor of a city waiting to be liberated. The very first shot, with the camera breaking through the clouds, like Hitler's aeroplane at the start of *Triumph of the Will*, is an aerial view of imperial Rome. This view, Scott says in a DVD commentary (without irony) 'is a model that he found in a museum down there'.[20] He means, of course, the model of imperial Rome commissioned by Mussolini for his great exhibition, which is still on display at the Museo della Civiltà Romana in Rome.[21] The camera sweeps over this and lands on an oversized eagle on a triumphal arch—again an echo of Riefenstahl's focus on the emblems of the Nazi regime. The assembled troops in the implausibly large forum evoke quite precisely the formations of the Nazi troops in the central square in front of Nuremberg's cathedral, also filmed from above. While the idea of equating imperial Rome with fascist Italy or Nazi Germany through the image of masses crowded into the city squares and screaming variations on 'Hail Caesar' is an old cinematic convention, this scene goes a step further in borrowing so directly from Riefenstahl. Quite starkly desaturated of colour, the scene evokes the black and white of newsreels of the 1930s, and of pictures of, for instance, the fascist mass gatherings in

Rome. While the red rose petals[22] and the children with their flower wreaths provide just enough colour to make the scene look beautiful, the overall effect is frigid and alienating, even for the viewer who is unaware of the deliberate borrowings from Nazi propaganda. Another significant influence on the look of Scott's Rome can be found in Albert Speer's designs for Hitler's new Reichskanzlei, with its huge, dark marble and mosaic halls, its oversized columns, its black and gold panelling.[23] Many of these details can be seen in Commodus' palace, and add, like the Riefenstahl echoes, to the impression of imperial Rome as a totalitarian state.

This is not Scott's only vision of Rome. When the gladiators approach the city some time later, we get a more conventional view of the pastoral surroundings, and of the city nestled in its hills. There is more colour too, notably the yellow-gold of a kind of sandstone, rather than the usual filmic convention of gleaming white marble. Once again the city looks quite different from its earlier cinematic self. Notably, there is much more height to the buildings both in the way they are filmed, and through the way that the gladiators' gaze travels up, especially when they catch sight of the Colosseum. This last is so far withheld from the spectator as a whole panorama—instead we share the protagonist's view of it as close and looming—but is shown as a mere fragment at the moment. In this scene, the fascistic open spaces seem to be replaced by a—perhaps more authentic—view of a crowded and over-built city. The inspiration for this tall narrow look for Rome came, according to the production designer Arthur Max, from Sir Lawrence Alma-Tadema's paintings with their emphasis on the height of columns and the narrow streets he favours for instance in *Spring* (see Fig. 4).[24]

Like Alma-Tadema *Gladiator*'s designers emphasised the authenticity of small details, such as jewels or crockery. These

4   Spring, *Sir Laurence Alma-Tadema.*
Image and copyright: Getty Museum, Los Angeles.

minutiae serve as signs of the historical authenticity of the film, while the bigger things are happily tampered with to achieve the desired overall effect. Modern editing demands that much more close-up work is included in final cuts (often with a view to how films will look on the television screen). This means that the small touches of authenticity can now be used in a way that used not to be possible. Indeed, David Bordwell notes in his work on contemporary Hollywood cinema how crammed with detail modern films are compared to older ones, a tendency he describes as 'worldmaking'.[25] As he says, it is striking how crowded with detail the sets of *Gladiator* are, compared to those of *Ben-Hur* or *Fall*.

Very little of *Gladiator*'s politics (such as it is) is conveyed by dialogue: style and design are really how this history of Rome is told. Where *Fall* and *Spartacus* have substantial debates in the Senate in which political positions are mapped out and conflicts discussed, Scott creates a world that looks totalitarian and anti-democratic by association. He contrasts this world with the small community of the gladiators, which soon takes on a paramilitary aspect, and with the 'dream that was Rome', associated mainly with a very vague sense of the moral uprightness of Derek Jacoby's senator Gracchus. Scott is often accused of making films that are slick and stylish, but morally empty.[26] Scott himself and his collaborators would refer to this preoccupation with design as 'creating worlds'. He is quoted as saying that *Gladiator* was unusual in that 'In this instance, the world came first, then the story'.[27] This chimes well with the idea that the initial inspiration came from the well-known and frequently reproduced painting by Jean-Léon Gérôme entitled *Pollice Verso* (or *Thumbs Down*) that depicts a scene in the Colosseum.

Scott's film includes one scene in the Senate only, and it is worth commenting on. First of all, it is apparent that the production design goes to some lengths to make this *not* look like a toga epic; of course, the Senate, with its inevitable clustering of toga-wearers is particularly dangerous territory. We have already looked at the effect of the unusual black borders on the senators' togas we see here. The garments also appear to be made of a very heavy wool that makes them look less like 'dressing-up'. They are also longer than the togas of the 1960s films, thus avoiding the display of sandals that might betray the film as, after all, an old-style historical epic. These aesthetically pleasing senators are never seen in any debating or counselling function, and indeed the room or building is not set out for debate. At first one has the impression that it looks like one of Albert Speer's huge corridors, framed by enormous columns. The camera then almost immediately cuts to Commodus, sitting on a throne, with senators grouped against a massive column behind him. A dialogue of sorts takes place between Gracchus and Commodus, but there is nothing of the kind of rhetoric we expect to see in this setting. These must be the least assertive senators in Rome's cinematic history, even if they are the most beautifully photographed.

Violence as spectacle: the German battle

One notices at once during the German battle that the very fast cutting combined with hand-held camera shots produces a somewhat disorienting effect, which makes it difficult to be certain exactly what one is seeing. This is a rather emphatic editing technique—not exactly in keeping with old-fashioned Hollywood principles of transparent narration. It might be seen as creating the impression of immediate contact with the action on the screen, but Scott's editing does not make events appear natural or realistic. The continuity of time and space are not always preserved, so the effect can be quite alienating. Rather than heighten realism, the fast and juxtaposed editing draws attention to artifice in quite a self-aware way, characteristic of what David Bordwell has described as 'intensified continuity'.[28]

The effect of the editing used in almost all the fight scenes in the arena is that the film viewer cannot comfortably occupy the position of the Roman spectators, because the act of viewing is too overt and self-conscious. We are too disoriented and made too aware of our position as spectators by all the visible camera and editing activity. It is an interesting and innovative approach for a historical film: clarity and didacticism, as well as seamless story-telling, are given up (at least momentarily) in favour of a more fragmented, doubtful—perhaps even questioning—approach. This uncertainty was described by one reviewer: 'chopped-off limbs, severed heads, gushing blood, etc., fly by so quickly that you can't be sure of what you saw, or whether indeed you saw it'.[29]

This view of Scott's spectacles of violence is worth considering alongside the more conventional view that all displays of violence are intended to arouse and 'hook' an audience with a view to nothing but the box-office return. So in the German battle we are bombarded with the briefest glimpses or fragments of action, often shocking in the extreme, but edited in such a visible and self-aware manner that it stuns us with the technical virtuosity of the spectacle. We catch glimpses of terrible violence and also, through the use of intermittent close-ups of details, a glimpse of 'history', or what is meant to look like history (weapons, helmets and the like, a standard once, the gritty and 'realistic'-looking faces and bodies of 'Romans' and 'Germans'). This is spectacle in the sense that it suspends narrative in favour of display, but it is also a form of display that is used to engage (and disorient, or shock) the viewer in an almost physical way. As a way of representing history it has none of the theatricality or staginess or the distanced didacticism of similar scenes in earlier films.

The arena: story and spectacle

The first of the gladiatorial fights in Africa is another excellent example of this way of filming. Of course, the unspeakable violence and gore has to be one of the selling points of this film; and it is clear that the fight sequences are high points of the film in terms of spectacle and display, and that they *do* suspend story-telling at times. The style of display here is again striking, and arguably makes the very thing it displays questionable.[30]

As the gladiators enter the arena out of the dark tunnel where they have been waiting, we (and they) are blinded by the sunlight that hits the camera as the doors open. The camera angle clearly invites us to identify not with the spectators but with the performers—and so resolves, or at least dilutes, the old dilemma of where we stand vis-à-vis Roman spectacles. Less than a second later, we see the mace and chain swing towards the camera and injure one of the gladiators in the most savage way. The camera stays very close to the action at all times, and once more, as in the German battle, the intercutting is fast and furious—it is almost impossible to keep track of what is happening to whom. Blood and sweat sprays at the camera, limbs are chopped off, knives delve into flesh; once more the violence is gut-wrenching, but often only fleetingly glimpsed. There are some cuts away to the impresario Proximo and his friends in the audience, but the points of view of the fight itself are almost exclusively extreme close-ups and very fragmentary. The feeling of disorientation is supplemented by a sense of being physically almost too close to the action. This effect of corporeal involvement is at least partly a result of the extreme aural effects (the sounds of slicing flesh, clanging shields, and bodies falling to the ground). The spectacle is both fascinating and repellent, indulging viewers' fascination with ever-escalating violence, and showing off the virtuosity with which the violence is made aesthetic. Elvis Mitchell describes it well in his review for the *New York Times*: 'With each scene composed for an audience's delectation of the constant slaughter, the movie is both pandering and detached. It's like a handsomely designed weapon: you can't take your eyes off it even though you may be repelled by its purpose'.[31]

In addition to this moral dislocation, the physical disorientation created by the loss of a stable and secure point of view and by the extreme sounds has implications for the historiography that *Gladiator* makes. By dispensing with narrative linearity in favour of corporeal engagement, this new film may be going a long way towards embracing the potential of film for making history 'come alive'. It certainly plunges the viewer right into things—that is why it is so important that Scott's spectacles, or displays, are filmed in this corporeally aggressive manner. Narrative linearity and secure points of view are lost, but the sense of 'being there' or in Rosenstone's words being 'prisoners of history' is very strong. The experience of this type of sensory assault in the cinema is familiar to any contemporary cinemagoer, but it is a relatively recent phenomenon. The film historian Thomas Elsaesser describes it as 'engulfment' and views it as a characteristic of the new, so-called 'post-classical' Hollywood in which special effects tend to leap out of the picture visually and aurally and cause the viewer to be disoriented and shocked.[32] This is underlined at the end of the sequence with the vertiginous camera moving in circles round and round the arena, not resting on any particular point, as if to underline Maximus' own disorientation and shock at what he has just done.

The problems associated with making a spectacle of violence in gladiatorial combat and in film are made explicit in the second arena sequence in Africa. Proximo is critical of Maximus' performance, because he is too efficient: 'All you do is kill, kill, kill. The crowd don't want a butcher, they want a hero. We want them to keep coming back. Don't just hack them to pieces. Remember you are an entertainer'. Only *Spartacus* went as far as this in making the protagonist's humiliation so explicit. It is usually more important to retain the hero's dignity by allowing the audience for the most part to ignore that aspect of their degradation, and the audience's complicity in it. But while *Gladiator* does make the hero's loss of status explicit in the spectacle, it uses narrative to help him compensate for it. When Maximus walks past the other gladiators on his way into the arena, he is saluted by them in a conscious echo of his inspection of the troops at the beginning of the film; thus his position as leader is re-established and the humiliation of being called an entertainer is ameliorated. There follows a virtuoso fight sequence, again very self-consciously edited, which ends with an excessively brutal killing, involving some flashy sword work.

After this performance, Maximus shifts out of his position as passive object of the spectators' gaze, lashing out at them with his own criticism of the spectacle he has offered. First though, he hurls one of his swords into the VIP enclosure, echoing Draba's similar act of defiance in *Spartacus*. But where Draba aims to kill and is executed, Maximus' challenge is rhetorical: 'Are you not entertained? Is this not why you're here?' Through this short sequence Scott has established a knowing self-awareness of the degradation represented by the spectacle and the protagonist's own contempt for it. He has also been able to provide another stunning display of stylishly edited violence that the viewer can enjoy all the more for being able still to see the hero as an active subject, rather than a degraded passive object.

The Carthaginian battle in the Colosseum works with similar manoeuvres, and is also a good example of how Scott innovates the filming of history. Much is made in this scene of the Colosseum itself, as the camera moves around the entire set (or rather a fragment of it, supplemented by a great deal of digital imagery), taking in its size, the crowds, the noise, and so on; this is a real 'epic' moment in its preoccupation with scale and splendour. In the Colosseum Maximus and his group are the 'Carthaginians', the other group of gladiators are the 'Romans'. Oddly, Scipio's 'Roman' legions consist of black quasi-Amazons, in gold armour, riding flashy chariots, while the group announced as the 'barbarian hordes' look remarkably like Roman soldiers, with their chain-mail shirts, dull metallic helmets, and identical black shields. This presentation, however bizarre, allows the spectator to believe in the fiction created by Maximus that the gladiators somehow act as a substitute Roman army. This, of course, is why they win the battle—so when Commodus comments on the apparent reversal of history, the real answer is that there has been none: people had merely been given the wrong parts to play. Maximus reversed the roles so that we have been watching a legitimate and brave group of Roman soldiers fight and defeat an undisciplined (female, black) group of savages. The grimmest acts of violence (slicing bodies in half, and such like) are perpetrated on the female warriors, while our heroic soldiers manage to save themselves by working effectively under Maximus' command. Inevitably, the viewer is keen for Maximus and his colleagues to survive; it is convenient therefore that we can root for Maximus as 'the general' (the other gladiators will address him thus from now on), rather than Maximus the entertainer. It is important to the evolution of the character, and to the development of the idea of spectacle in the film that Maximus asserts himself in the Colosseum as a strong military leader, rather than as a mere gladiator. This gives the viewer the necessary narrative justification for enjoying the spectacle.

The even more gratuitous display offered in the tiger sequence is ameliorated also by being represented as a mere test for the real political battle to be fought. Maximus has the opportunity to voice his political standpoint—thus seizing a subject position and the moral high ground—before he enters the arena. This sets the tone for the battle: 'Marcus Aurelius had a dream of Rome, Proximo. This is not it'. Together with our protagonist we can feel contempt for the ecstatic mob, but we can take pleasure in the thrill and the technical brilliance of the fight too, especially because we are rooting for the right cause all the time: the abolition of the society of spectacle and tyranny for which the Colosseum acts as a powerful metonym. It is also clear, from the personal interest shown by both Commodus and the senators that this fight is a political event rather than the spectacle the audience in the arena thinks it is. Commodus hints that he has arranged for the assassination of Maximus, whom he clearly views as more than a slave and gladiator. Thus we are very much aware of the engagement of the individual spectators: the senator Gracchus, who hopes to enlist Maximus for his cause; the emperor, who hopes to have his rival assassinated; Lucilla, who has political aspirations for Maximus; and the servant Cicero, who will become instrumental in the plot to overthrow Commodus. By frequently cutting away from the arena to the individual spectators, Scott presents the gladiatorial spectacle as an event with political and historical significance. Because of all this political interest in the fight the narrative is not suspended in this scene of violence. Maximus continues to be a significant agent in the story rather than becoming a mere object of display. Unusually, the viewer is able to experience visual pleasure through the arena spectacle *without* necessarily siding with Rome and tyranny. When Maximus takes the decision to spare Tigris it is clear that this was *his* show, after all, not Commodus'.

After the fight Commodus and Maximus have their very personal encounter in the arena, surrounded by the Praetorian Guards, whose circle creates a kind of mini-arena, reinforcing Maximus' status and eroding the boundary between the emperor as spectator and the gladiator as entertainer.

Three salient characteristics emerge from the spectacular fight sequences that punctuate *Gladiator*. First, they are filmed in a way that draws attention to the technical skill of the display and so may create a sense of critical self-awareness for the viewer. Second, the techniques of shock and corporeal engulfment mean that the spectator experiences a relatively direct engagement with the brutality on display. Third, each scene of violence is embedded in the narrative in a range of ways that avoid objectifying the protagonist. As a result of all this, the separation between story and spectacle that is a characteristic of earlier epic films is not so keenly felt in *Gladiator* and this may add to its modernity and to its acceptability for a contemporary audience.

Scott also shows a very sharp sense of what it might mean to present history in images rather than words. *Gladiator* embraces the entire arsenal of contemporary Hollywood's techniques and scrupulously avoids the theatricality and textual ponderousness associated with its predecessors' cinematic antiquity. The result is a 'lively' sense of the past—inaccurate, undoubtedly, but engrossing. To a large part this success is a result of Scott's ability to bridge the gulf between story and spectacle.

CHAPTER 6

FELLINI SATYRICON
'FAREWELL TO ANTIQUITY' OR 'DAILY LIFE IN ANCIENT ROME'?

F*ellini Satyricon*, Federico Fellini's widescreen Roman spectacle filmed at Rome's Cinecittà like *Ben-Hur* and *Cleopatra*, was released in 1969. It could not be further away from the stories and the spectacles of the Rome of *The Fall of the Roman Empire* or *Spartacus*, or any number of its Italian predecessors. Based on parts of Petronius' fragmentary novel, the film depicts the two young protagonists, Encolpio and Ascilto, in a series of more or less unfortunate events, set vaguely in imperial Rome, around the Bay of Naples and further afield in the empire. Like the text that inspired it, *Fellini Satyricon* parodies the idea of the epic quest by replacing the persecuted Odysseus or Aeneas with the figure of Encolpio, a rather low-rent character occupied by some rather prosaic quests (first the loss of a young male lover, then the curing of a temporary sexual dysfunction). To some extent *Fellini Satyricon* sets itself up to be the opposite of Cinecittà and Hollywood versions of ancient Rome. Indeed, Fellini frequently said that *Satyricon* was inspired by the movies he saw in his childhood. In making up his own cinematic ancient world, Fellini has broken up the cinematic clichés of columns, bathhouses, toga-clad emperors and sexually voracious patrician ladies, and overlaid them with the patina of age and decay. Faces and buildings are ruined, cracked and tired—not the shiny reconstructions of historical epic.

Fellini Satyricon **and art cinema**

In many ways, *Fellini Satyricon* conforms to the characteristics of the art film of the 1960s and early 1970s as formulated by David Bordwell in an essay of 1979.[1] The protagonists lack the clearly defined characters and objectives of mainstream narrative cinema; the film's itinerary is not defined by a clear goal and tends towards the episodic or picaresque. This is very much true of Encolpio, whose vague itinerary and opaque or non-existent decision-making are noticeable very early on, after the loss of Gitone. A strong hint of the protagonists' lack of definition comes when the three young men, wandering around the tenement buildings at night, stop to ask one of the old hags if she knows where they live. Encolpio and Ascilto's lack of visible sympathy or reaction to the suicides at the villa is another example of their loosely defined characters. Although the idea of regaining Gitone is a dominant driving force at the start of the film (in Encolpio's opening speech and his assertion of ownership of Gitone at Vernacchio's theatre), the urgency soon peters out and is then replaced with the idea of curing Encolpio's impotence.

Fellini Satyricon also gives prominence to its author, as its full title demonstrates. The vision and the story we are seeing on the screen is controlled by him and by his imagination rather than by the demands of a studio or the hallmarks of a genre. In art film stylistic 'trademark' features are frequent reminders of the author's presence; in *Satyricon* we see, for instance, Fellini's well-known preoccupation with spectacle (in the theatre scene, in the gladiatorial mime, in Trimalchio's feast) and his penchant for grotesque human figures (the many extras, but also the hermaphrodite and the strange little emperor). These features are ways of reminding us that this may be ancient Rome, but it is Fellini's ancient Rome.

In defining itself as revolutionary or avant-garde, art cinema generally rejects the conventions of verisimilitude and 'seamlessness' that help mainstream film to reconcile the dual forces of narrative and spectacle. *Satyricon*, like most art film, makes a point of highlighting temporal, spatial, and causal ambiguity. For instance, we cannot tell how Encolpio arrives at the art gallery after the earthquake, and we are unsure how Eumolpo escapes from the furnace at Trimalchio's villa. In most films of this type, the ambiguity is characteristic of a certain type of realism (just as in life, we are rarely certain why decisions are made or why certain things happen) or of a way of highlighting the author's subjectivity (as narrator, the director decides not to let you know how a character arrived at a particular place or decision). In *Satyricon*, the principles of ambiguity and incomprehension are extended further. The film is based on the idea that we are piecing a narrative together from fragments, and observing an alien world peopled by characters we do not understand and who act in ways that we cannot interpret. For example, it is unclear what the audience at Vernacchio's theatre are up to with their bizarre facial gymnastics; the linguistic and visual confusion of the *subura* scene is impossible to penetrate; the significance of the eccentric jumping up and down in the candle-lit bath performed just before Trimalchio's party is anybody's guess; Fortunata's elaborate gesticulations during the banquet are equally opaque.

However, the art cinema of the 1960s defined itself predominantly as a cinema of realism (for example in the major movements of Neorealism and the Nouvelle Vague). This included the kind of features praised by Bazin that we have discussed above (realistic representations of time and space, for instance with long takes, moving cameras, and so on). The brand of realism espoused by art cinema also included, in most cases, a commitment to psychologically complex characters. Here Fellini can be seen to part company with his artistic colleagues: the fundamental principle of incomprehension and fragmentation that governs *Satyricon* means that the protagonists are inscrutable to such a degree that they appear shallow. The dubbing process, deliberately and obviously out of sync with lip movements (often the actors are speaking English and are dubbed into Italian), increases the impression that these characters have no psychological depth at all. The alienation that results from this is what Fellini says he wanted for the film, but it is also the feature that film critics and reviewers found most difficult to come to terms with.

Finally, the open ending is a frequent, if not obligatory, feature of the art film. *Satyricon*, with its mid-sentence ending, is a kind of master-class in open-endedness. Again, helped by the fragmentary status of its model, this film goes further than some in highlighting the fact that the film is only a part of the story. Not only does the narration simply cease in mid-sentence, but the final freezing of Encolpio's features into the image of a fresco painting on a ruined fragment of wall on a deserted island concludes the film with the assertion that all we have access to from the ancient past are isolated images. What we have seen was just a glimpse of what might have been, not a classical story with a clear trajectory and a clear conclusion. Finally, the inscrutability of antiquity is what the viewer is left with as the ancient painted faces gaze out at us.

Classicists today are enthusiastic about Fellini's depiction of an unfamiliar antiquity, characterised as fragmentary, inspired by the image of the ruin or the crumbling fresco.[2] Fellini himself commented on it widely in interviews and in his own writing; he may indeed, as Jon Solomon puts it, have 'amused himself by stretching the philosophy and meaning of *Satyricon*'.[3] Much of what the director said and wrote has become established as part of the film's cultural status, especially including his many mentions of his approach to antiquity as a 'dream', as a 'fragment', and as a form of 'archaeology'.[4] This rejection of reconstruction and of narrative in favour of a keen interest in the ruin and the fragment is an attractive alternative to the finished stories of mainstream movies. It is also, as has been shown, entirely in keeping with a long tradition of antiquarian interest in the city of Rome and in the ways in which it displays the traces of its past.[5] The historical epics' stories and spectacles are all informed by the desire to recreate, as realistically as possible, what it might have been like to be in Rome during the time of the Caesars. Fellini, by contrast, says that he aims to show what it is like to look upon the past from a very long way away, without being fully able to understand it.

Among film critics, Pauline Kael is perhaps alone in finding *Fellini Satyricon* a deeply conservative view of the ancient world, comparable, in her view, with the spectacles of Cecil B. de Mille. She saw Fellini's obsession with Roman decadence and corruption as indicative of a moral and emotional conservatism that was fundamentally Christian in character.[6] There may be some justification for this view. There are some aspects of the film, and a plethora of statements made by the director that indicate a rather more conventional attitude to imperial Roman society than one might associate with an avant-garde filmmaker like Fellini. In his preoccupation with Roman decadence and the parallels he draws between that decadence and the dissolution of his own age, Fellini appears to betray a mixture of fascination with and moral outrage at the depravity of the ancient Romans. This attitude is, of course, exactly the prurient fascination joined with moral righteousness that characterises Roman epic movies such as those of de Mille. So, when Fellini wrote in *Playboy* magazine a lavishly illustrated essay on his new feature, there is more than a hint of prurience in the assertion that:

> it was not possible to ignore the obvious analogy between the Roman society described by Petronius—corrupt, dissolute, cynical—and the society of today, at the height of its magnificence but already revealing the signs of a progressive decay; a society where every religious, philosophic, ideological and social belief has crumbled, leaving in its place a sick, frenetic occultism, an impotent promiscuity.[7]

Fellini on Fellini: before Christianity

Fellini enjoyed talking and writing about his film, often teasing critics and scholars a little with quite outrageous claims. Comments and reflections on *Satyricon* can be found in any number of interviews and collections of Fellini's writings; the main sources I have looked at here are published in Dario Zanelli's book *Fellini's Satyricon*, which contains the screenplay, alongside Fellini's own preface to the 'treatment' (a draft outline of the film that does not entirely correspond with the finished product), and a conversation between the Italian novelist Alberto Moravia and Fellini himself, which was first published in British *Vogue* around the time of the film's release. This dialogue, entitled 'Documentary of a Dream', contributed much to establishing the cult status of *Fellini Satyricon*. Six months or so after the *Vogue* feature, Moravia also published an essay in the *New York Review of Books*, 'Dreaming up Petronius', in which he came up with the description of the film as a 'farewell to antiquity'.

Shortly before fully embarking on the Petronius project, Fellini made a film for NBC Television, which, under the title *A Director's Notebook* (1969), purports in part to document the story of the preparatory work for *Satyricon*. It contains some fantastical sequences that anticipate some of the scenes in the later film *Roma* (1972), and some actual documentary sequences, including a series of audition interviews with people who wanted to be in *Satyricon*. *Director's Notebook* is very much a part of the discourse surrounding *Satyricon* that added to its prominence. Together the NBC television film and the pieces in *Playboy*, *Vogue* and the *New York Review of Books* can be seen to build up an image of the film as a highbrow, intellectual, and highly personal engagement with antiquity.

Given all its avant-garde intellectual credentials, it is surprising perhaps to find that in the *Playboy* essay mentioned above, Federico Fellini describes the moment when his vision for *Satyricon* emerged by evoking one of the oldest Roman touristic clichés—a visit to the Colosseum by night: [8] 'Then one night, in the Colosseum, I saw that horrendous lunar catastrophe of stone, that immense skull devoured by time, as the testimony of a civilization with a different destiny, and it communicated to me for one instant a shiver of terror and of delight'.[9] With its evocation of the moonlit structure as an emblem of Rome's decadence (the horror, the pleasurable shiver of fear) and ruin (the skull devoured by time), Fellini's setting of the scene brings to mind the long tradition of moonlit Colosseum visits, all tinged with the shadow of corruption and decay that hovers over the monument. Elsewhere in the *Playboy* essay, Fellini is quite scornful of the image and its associations and he was shrewd enough to omit the Colosseum completely from the finished film.[10] The gladiatorial games featured in the initial draft treatment do not appear in the film itself.

The building makes a pivotal appearance, however, in *A Director's Notebook*. At the very moment when Fellini begins, in voice-over narration, to talk of his new project (which he describes here as 'a voyage in time'), we see on the screen the Colosseum, lit up at night. The building is surrounded by the flow of traffic on the Via dei Fori Imperiali; it is an image that anticipates the juxtaposition of past and present that Fellini exploits more fully in *Roma* (1972).[11] The American narrator tells us that Fellini has come to the Colosseum ('this half-world of Rome in the small hours') at the start of his new film to study the 'night-wanderers, looking for parallels between modern Rome and Nero's Rome'. Petronius himself, the narrator tells us in a mock-documentary tone, used to come here to observe 'ancient counterparts of these same, shadowy individuals'. Fellini's camera then shows a motley collection of figures: some gangsters, some homeless people and some striking transvestites possibly looking for business. Some, if not all, of this nocturnal activity might have been staged for Fellini's purposes, but the rather seedy ambience does seem to have some grounding in contemporary reality. It appears that, once 'official' moonlit tourist visits to the Colosseum ceased to be possible, the site became a popular nocturnal hang-out for the gay community, and seems to have remained so up until the 1980s when the area was more securely fenced with metal gates.[12] For Fellini's purposes, the Colosseum's status as an emblem of Rome's eternity, mixed with its modern transformation into a meeting place for illicit sexual encounters, makes it a perfect locus for reflecting on decadence past and present.[13]

In part the Colosseum is also a key aspect of a more conservative vision of Rome that owes something to the stock themes of decadence and cruelty that can be found both in the old movies and in history books. Its use as an introduction to Fellini's vision of Rome also serves to highlight the focus on spectacle (rather than story-telling) that in fact typifies both *Satyricon* and later *Roma*. For Fellini, the Colosseum is emblematic not only of ancient Rome itself, but also of the Rome of the movies. The scenes that most encapsulate cinematic Rome for Fellini are those visions of toga-clad, cruelly twisted emperors presiding over gladiatorial spectacles. The Colosseum is then both a reminder of Roman decadence and a potent symbol of spectatorship itself. As Fellini puts it in a letter outlining his purpose for *Satyricon*: 'Satyricon, which is set in the Rome of decadence, brings back memories of the very origins of the cinema . . . And this is the first time that I can recreate, in my own way, with a lucid amusement, my first feelings as a spectator'.[14]

In 'Documentary of a Dream', the conversation with Alberto Moravia, Fellini expands on his fascination with the ancient Romans' love of gladiatorial games.[15] Here we sense that there is a moralising dimension to the director's interest in the games:

> When I think that at the time of Hadrian, the cultivated, sensitive, cosmopolitan emperor . . . in the Colosseum at Rome one could witness the massacre of seventy-five pairs of gladiators in a single afternoon . . . What escapes us is the mentality of a world in which you went to the box office of a theatre and bought a ticket which entitled you to entertain yourself with the agony of a fellow human being killed by the sword or devoured by a wild beast.[16]

Moravia, in a deft move, points out to Fellini that the practices he describes came to an end with the arrival of Christianity. He goes on to suggest to Fellini that he is in fact unwittingly interpreting ancient Rome as the antithesis of Christian purity.[17]

Fellini is annoyed to find his attitude to antiquity likened to Christian fear and condemnation of the sins of pagan Rome, when he claims to have 'tried to look at pagan Rome with eyes not obscured by the myths and ideologies that have succeeded each other throughout two thousand years of history'.[18] Despite these protestations, Moravia asserts in an essay published after the film's release that he feels his first judgement is confirmed, having seen the film, and that Fellini's antiquity is corrupt and moribund, and that the director is immensely attracted by the 'most celebrated and most historic of all decadences'.[19]

Fellini remarks variously on the 'absence of Christ' from his film, which is also a feature of the advertising slogan 'Rome. Before Christ. After Fellini' (see Fig. 5). This promises decadence and excess in an attempt to get audiences into the movie theatre; it also hints at the salvation story that audiences perhaps expect from a film set in ancient Rome; it attributes to Fellini himself both the role of the saviour, and of the provider of the lavish spectacle of imperial Rome. While Fellini never says that pagan Rome needed Christianity to heal itself, he does describe the world he creates for the film as a society 'waiting for something new', and he seems to attribute some of the sexual and violent excesses to the absence of Christian morality.[20] His historical consultant, Luca Canali, is quoted as saying that Fellini views as a central issue in the *Satyricon* 'the presentiment of collapse, the end of a civilization which is breaking up from the spiritual point of view'.[21] The director himself describes Petronius' society in this way:

> In fact it seems we can find disconcerting analogies between Roman society before the final arrival of Christianity—a cynical society, impassive, corrupt and frenzied—and society today ... Then as now we find ourselves confronting a society at the height of its

5   *Poster for* Fellini Satyricon.
*Image from author's own
collection. Copyright: MGM.*

splendor but revealing already the signs of progressive dissolution.[22]

The juxtaposition of that 'height of splendor' with the decay that is setting in is cast from the same mould as the opening statements of *Spartacus* or *The Fall of the Roman Empire*. In this fundamentally pessimistic view of imperial Rome, Fellini is not so very far removed from the tradition he purports to spurn.

Fellini on Fellini: dreams and fragments

The idea of *Satyricon* as a dream is first articulated in 'Documentary of a Dream'. Here Fellini describes his approach to creating his ancient world, in a much-quoted passage:

> I've tried first of all to eliminate what is generally called
> history. That is to say, really, the idea that the ancient
> world 'actually' existed. Thus the atmosphere is not
> historical but that of a dream world. The ancient world
> perhaps never existed, but there is no doubt that we
> have dreamt it ... *Satyricon* should have the enigmatic
> transparency, the indecipherable clarity of dreams.[23]

Elsewhere, he talks variously about his detachment in
constructing his vision of imperial Rome, and about his desire
to show a form of antiquity that is entirely unfamiliar, alien, and
incomprehensible. This insistence on the obscurity of antiquity
marks the greatest difference between Fellini's Rome and the
Rome of mainstream historical spectacle. The most striking
example of this uncertainty is perhaps the use of strange facial
gestures, often directed straight at the camera. The weird
winking, tongue-wagging, and random gesturing are a kind of
'code' that the viewer is unable to decipher. Fellini describes this
sense of strangeness in the preface to the 'Treatment':

> Sometimes the customs of these characters must appear
> to us totally incomprehensible, some of their extravagant
> gestures as indecipherable: grimaces, winks and other
> codes whose meaning we have lost. We no longer know
> the allusions behind them ... as if we were watching a
> documentary on some Amazon Basin tribe.[24]

In his essay, 'Dreaming up Petronius', Moravia returns to
this dominant theme of alienation from the ancient world in
Fellini Satyricon. He develops here the idea that, as the latest in
a series of rebirths of antiquity, Fellini's film is 'somewhat like a
farewell'—that is, not a reconstruction but a taking apart, and
taking leave of the very idea of 'antiquity' as a familiar place or
notion:

> In what way does this very last of the Renaissances bid
> farewell to antiquity? That is, in what way does Fellini,
> in his movie, bid farewell to Petronius' world? He does so
> by finding it obscure, incomprehensible, half-obliterated,
> absurd, mysterious, dream-like ... For Fellini antiquity
> is a dream whose meaning has been lost, while still being
> there and making its presence felt at all times.[25]

Together, Moravia's interview with Fellini and the subsequent essay consolidate the view that *Satyricon* is a serious
attempt at discarding the kind of historical detail and emotional
engagement that is part and parcel of historical spectacle, and
that the result is a novel and original vision of Roman society. Much is made, too, of the idea of the fragment, and of the
ruin, again sustaining an interpretation of the film as *not* a historical film, as the opposite of a reconstruction.[26] This view is
supported by the fact that textual sources and scholarship are
somehow sidelined in many of Fellini's statements, while the
image of the fresco or of archaeological remains are frequently
evoked.[27] Moravia's interpretation of Fellini's approach is
especially perceptive when he explains Fellini's avoidance of
historical specificity:

> But how does Fellini avoid, indeed ignore, the rich
> knowledge we have of antiquity? ... by overlooking all
> that has been 'written' about antiquity and adhering to
> what has been 'depicted.' And he does this ... because
> very little remains of ancient painting and that little
> fragmentary, incomplete, and therefore mysterious.[28]

Moravia goes on to discuss how Fellini, rather than deal in
the sort of naturalistic reconstruction that is characteristic
of historical epic, has us gaze upon a world that is influenced
by the archaeological remains of its own representations. This

contemplation of antiquity as a ruin is finally how Moravia sees Fellini's project as 'taking leave of antiquity'.

This approach is first visualised in *A Director's Notebook*, in a scene set in the Roman metro; it is a sketch for the more famous underground excavation scene in *Roma*. In the striking scene in *Director's Notes* Fellini and his team are travelling on the metro in Rome with a 'Professor of Archaeology'. The professor introduces the idea of the 'traces' and 'layers' of an earlier Rome that are present in the subway's tunnels. As the train travels through the dark the professor acts as a kind of guide, explaining in his quaintly precise English tones all the different archaeological sites it passes through. Immediately after Fellini himself remarks that they are 'making a trip in time rather than space', the camera (and the travellers) notice that the station signs are in Latin, and that the platforms are occupied entirely by men and women in Roman costume. At first, these figures are quite still, some posed like statues, but then they begin to address the camera in incomprehensible or mumbled Latin, and to make the mysterious, opaque gestures and grimaces we see in *Satyricon*. Indeed, a number of the characters encountered here in the subway will be guests at Trimalchio's party or at Vernacchio's theatre in *Satyricon*.

This strange process of contemplating the faces of antiquity is in a sense reversed at the end of *Satyricon* when Encolpio and his young entourage become frozen into antique images as the film ends 'covered with the dust of centuries. It is all transformed into an antique fresco; a discolored fresco in Pompeiian colors.'[29] Instead of looking back at us, these ancient figures are now just lifeless images, entirely inscrutable. In *Roma*, Fellini continues to develop the theme when the frescos discovered in the metro turn out first to resemble many of the living characters who are gazing at them, and then to crumble and vanish as soon as they are discovered.

For Alberto Moravia, this final scene of *Satyricon* confirms the sense that Fellini's 'intuition' to discard written sources in favour of pictorial remains is the key to the film's character as a farewell to antiquity.

Fellini and 'daily life in ancient Rome'

Moravia claims that he takes Fellini at his word when he says he has never read anything.[30] And yet, it is clear even from his own discussions that the director has read a great deal and is aware of a number of textual influences. Fellini himself acknowledges, in the preface to the 'Treatment' (the initial outline of the film's structure) published by Zanelli, the presence of Apuleius and Horace's *Satires*, and his reading of Suetonius.[31] In addition, J.P. Sullivan has shown in detail how the 'ambience' of Fellini's Rome is influenced by a range of ancient literary sources.[32] Sullivan also points out the importance of Jerome Carcopino's popular book *Daily Life in Ancient Rome*, first published in French in 1939, and available in Italian translation in 1941.[33] I would suggest that these written sources were as important to Fellini's Rome as the more talked about 'fresco' vision. Carcopino was not only an excellent mine of information for Fellini and his researchers, but I suspect that Carcopino's view of imperial Rome as a society at the height of its powers and yet deeply decadent and ripe for salvation also had a strong influence on Fellini. For instance, it is clear that Fellini had read Carcopino's chapter on 'Shows and Spectacles', which is not only vividly imagined and detailed, but also rich in moralizing conclusions such as this: 'The conquering gospel taught the Romans no longer to tolerate the inveterate shame . . . Roman Christianity thus blotted out the crime against humanity which under the pagan Caesars had disgraced the amphitheatre of the empire.'[34]

Carcopino's influence on some of the detail of the film can be seen, for instance, in the opening scenes in the 'Treatment', which include a number of gladiatorial fights. While these are not ultimately realised in the film, they are excellent examples of the influence of Carcopino's book on Fellini's imagination. For instance, Fellini suggests a fight between an Amazon and dwarf where Carcopino has 'dwarf against woman', Fellini has fights between 'blacks and blacks', borrowed from Carcopino's 'Negro against Negro'. Like Carcopino's, Fellini's onlookers shout out the well-worn phrases, *ure*, *habet*, *verbera*.[35] The prostitutes under the archways mentioned by Fellini are in Carcopino's description of the Circus Maximus (where Fellini imagines the gladiatorial shows taking place).[36] It is of course to Fellini's credit that in the final version his film begins more imaginatively with Encolpio's monologue before the graffiti-covered wall—a far more original and striking image of Fellini's alien and fragmentary antiquity.

A good example of the palpable remains of Carcopino's influence is the rather repellent scene at Vernacchio's theatre (see Fig. 6), an illustration of the influence of Martial's epigrams on some of the most violent mimes, and on the interchangeability of theatre and arena that Carcopino highlights:

> As the mime reached the height of its achievement, it drove humanity as well as art off the Roman stage. It plumbed the depths of a perversion which had conquered the masses of the capital. They were not sickened by such exhibitions because the ghastly butcheries of the amphitheatre had long since debased their feelings and perverted their instincts.[37]

Carcopino's final example of the depravity of such spectacle, the performance of Mucius Scaevola's sacrifice of his hand is mentioned as one of the 'most terrifying mimes' presented in the

6   *Vernacchio's mime in* Fellini Satyricon.
Image from author's own collection. Copyright: MGM.

arena.[38] A version of this scene (in which the hand is amputated rather than burned) forms the gory climax of the scene on Vernacchio's makeshift stage and helps to signal the corruption and decadence of the society represented on Fellini's screen.[39]

But *Satyricon* is not entirely devoid of admirable Romans. The most notable instance is of course the Villa of the Suicides, very broadly based on the deaths of Aulus Caecina Paetus and his wife Arria, celebrated by Pliny and Martial and related at some length in Carcopino's chapter on the Roman matron.[40] In the film the suicide and the brief scene that precedes it are a rare oasis of calm and luminosity, a respite from the relentless frenzy that characterises most of the episodes. Here we come closer to the classical ideal of antiquity—rejected almost throughout the remainder of the film—than at any other moment. In the 'Treatment', Fellini envisages the villa as 'a noble building, constructed along the pure lines of classical architecture . . . It is luxurious, but discreetly so, and elegant'. The emphasis on purity, nobility, and discretion is striking and it is successfully realised. Against the stark but elegant backdrop of the villa, neither parents nor children display any of the strange gesturing and grimacing that other characters in the film indulge in. There are no thick layers of make-up, extravagant hairstyles, or extreme jewellery and colours. This family is the very image of ideal Roman patricians, a little reminiscent of the Christian family of aristocratic Romans seen at the start of *Quo Vadis*. Fellini's couple are, of course, meant to be Stoics, not Christians, but it seems that Fellini's interpretation is influenced by Carcopino's praise of the matron Arria, where an explicit connection is made between the moral superiority of Arria and her like and the early Christian martyrs: 'Thanks to such women, proud and free as Arria, ancient Rome, in the very years when she was about to receive the bloody baptism of the first Christian martyrs, scaled one of the loftiest moral heights humanity has conquered.'[41]

Fellini claimed that the scene was meant to allude to Petronius himself and his wife committing suicide, but the details and the atmosphere, as well as the implicit approval of the matron's dignity and calm are owed to Pliny's Arria, most likely via Carcopino. It is interesting that this scene is the only moment in the film when ancient Romans are observed with sympathy, perhaps even admiration. The wife recites Hadrian's well-known epigram on death, in one of the few moments of recognisable Latin. She is marked as admirable by this connection with Hadrian, who—for Fellini and Carcopino—stood for the cultured and civilised image of Rome as opposed to its decadence and depravity. In all, the scene stands out as a 'highbrow' moment in the otherwise seedy and decrepit atmosphere of the film. It is also noticeable as a moment in which ancient Romans act in the ways in which we expect them to, and live in an environment we recognise as 'Roman'. As an amalgamation of the stories of Arria and Paetus, and Petronius himself, with Hadrian's dying words thrown in, this scene is in the best tradition of historical film: research has been conducted, digested, and creatively shaped to tell a good story. The use of written sources and the influence of other films is undeniable, and makes questionable Fellini's and Moravia's insistence on this film as entirely the 'documentary of a dream'.

Fellini Satyricon and history film

The heightened sense of ambiguity that dominates Fellini's film is in many ways a long way removed from the six key characteristics of historical film drama set out by Rosenstone that we discussed in the introduction. But, surprisingly perhaps, *Satyricon* does not reject all of the conventions of historical feature film. So, for instance, its story is embedded in a wider perspective on historical events in a manner that is at times reminiscent of the mainstream films we have examined. Like *Fall*, *Satyricon* ends on a note of pessimism for Rome's fate as the friends of Eumolpo sit down to their cannibalistic feast, observed and then abandoned by the younger generation. Encolpio and the other young people, in turning away from the grotesque decadence of their elders with a glimpse of what is to come (the final words of the film are 'in years to come . . .') turn their backs on Rome in a move that parallels Livius and Lucilla's departure from the auctioning of the emperor's title. Indeed, the protagonists' rejection of the Roman way of life is almost a prerogative of such films, as can be seen in Judah Ben-Hur's near-conversion to Christianity, in the departure of Varinia and her baby at the end of *Spartacus*, and of course in Maximus' death and departure for the world of the dead in *Gladiator*. In all these cases, the idea of progress, as Rosenstone has put it, dominates the narrative: Rome may be decaying and corrupt, but out of its ashes something better is going to rise. In some cases, this improvement is quite narrowly defined as the rise of Christianity (*Quo Vadis*, *Ben-Hur*), in others it is the end of slavery (*Spartacus*, *Gladiator*). In *Satyricon*, there is a feeling that Christianity does hover somewhere over the end, but it is diluted by a sense that the future lies in the innocence and energy of youth.

Rosenstone's second characteristic of history film is its concentration on individuals. Historical events are always, in historical feature films, presented through the story of their effect on specific individuals: slavery affects the freedom of Spartacus and Varinia to marry and raise a family, Roman domination of the east affects Judah and his family, and his friendship with Messala, and so on. In *Satyricon*, there is no big historical event or movement, but the general corruption and decay of the Roman Empire is seen through its effects on Encolpio and Ascilto. However, these individuals are not sufficiently clearly or sympathetically portrayed, and their reactions to events are so ambiguous that they cannot be said to carry the narrative, or to help the viewer to make sense of the represented past. In *Satyricon*, the protagonists only contribute to the sense of alienation and incomprehension that dominates the film's representation of antiquity.

The third of Rosenstone's factors, that the events of the past are portrayed in mainstream drama as completed, and their interpretation as clear and unambiguous, is clearly not the case for *Satyricon*. Of course, this is not a film about any concrete historical event or era, which in itself makes it quite incompatible with the generic demands of historical drama. However, some of the things that happen in the film conform to the types of events one might see in a historical feature film about imperial Rome. For instance, there is the murder of the emperor and the subsequent triumphal procession, and the suicides of the patrician couple. None of these events is motivated or explained. It is possible that the suicides are a direct result of the change of regime, but this is never stated.

Fourth, in historical feature films, the past is always represented in a way that draws the spectator into events emotionally, creating the impression of participation rather than observation. Fellini's insistence on the remoteness and inaccessibility of the ancient world makes this kind of experience impossible. His camera pretends to observe the baffling events, but it is scarcely possible for the viewer to find a character to identify with or to sympathise with. For example, the events on Lichas' boat are repellent, but the ostensible victims are not drawn clearly enough for us to care about them, nor is their potential anguish made explicit. Emotional identification is never encouraged in this film, where the protagonist himself is mostly a detached observer. Encolpio's own mission, to find a cure for his sexual dysfunction, is too absurd to be taken seriously. Any attempt to empathise or identify with the characters is in any case thwarted by the dubbing process: Encolpio's lips move in English while the soundtrack delivers plaintive Italian. There is no chance of absorption into this cinematic world, which does its very best to make itself unapproachable and alien.

Finally, it is worth discussing the way in which Fellini's film creates the 'look' of the past through landscape, buildings, dress, and objects, as well as the human body. In this aspect, if in no other, *Satyricon* comes close to fulfilling the criteria of a historical feature film. The ancient Rome Fellini has created does not have much affinity with our world today: it is entirely devoid of the familiar touches that often characterise historical film. It never does much to pander to the idea that 'humanity is always the same'. Fellini has created a world that looks and feels distinctly other, and remote. There are many traces of historical authenticity—the little tunics worn by the young slaves, the women's elaborate hairstyles, some of the food at Trimalchio's villa, some of the artworks in the gallery and in the villa, the death-masks in the villa, and Vernacchio's mime are all examples. The fabrics, metals, and leather worn by most of the characters are also made to look as authentically Roman as those in mainstream history films, if not more so. The colour scheme at Trimalchio's party is clearly inspired by Pompeian wall-paintings. As in any historical feature there is also much that is invented (the swing in the brothel, the strange candle-lit mass bathing) or inspired by later artworks (such as the pretty garlanded boys, who could be straight out of Alma-Tadema's *Spring*). Fellini's use of the human body to create his worlds is legendary; in *Satyricon* it is the faces of the actors who bring ancient Rome to life: the dirty pretty features of Martin Potter and street-wise viciousness of Hiram Keller evoke contemporary hippy culture just by their presence on the screen. And yet, dressed in their short tunics, they become entirely part of the remote world of antiquity. In this world, Joseph Wheeler's suicidal aristocrat looks uncannily like an Egyptian mummy portrait, and Magali Noel's costume as Fortunata is a good likeness of the portrait busts of imperial Roman women. Other characters, such as the emperor, the hermaphrodite, the nymphomaniac, and the masses of unsavoury inhabitants of the tenement blocks add to the sense of a real world in which human beings were different and often very strange. In part, this is true of all of Fellini's cinematic worlds, but combined with the historical detail, this world is very definitely ancient and Roman.

This chapter began by recognising that the ideas of spectacle and spectatorship are key catalysts for Fellini's cinematic Rome. Throughout his career Fellini was intrigued by spectacle and especially by spectacle as divorced from story or narrative— as in the circus or variety show, or at the fair. In *Satyricon* he indulges this fascination while at the same time parodying the Roman historical movies' own preoccupation with showing off the spectacular decadence of imperial Rome. The rejection of a strong story only adds to the sense that, as in Fellini's next film, *Roma*, in *Satyricon* 'The only unity of Rome is that of the spectacle'.[42]

CHAPTER 7

TITUS

ROME AND THE PENNY ARCADE

Described by one critic as an 'unsettling conflation of imperial and fascist Rome, with more than a dash of Las Vegas glamour',[1] *Titus* (1999), released shortly before *Gladiator*, creates an entirely new Roman world and brings to a head a number of the key issues that we have identified in this study of cinematic Rome. In some places, the world of *Titus* is an interpretation of the city of Rome itself, in others it is made up of other cinematic Roman worlds; in some parts it is Shakespeare's world, in others it visualises Latin texts and reinterprets works of art. It is certainly the most complex and probably the most self-aware of the cinematic stories and spectacles of Rome that are discussed here.

Shakespeare's shocking and dark historical fiction, *Titus Andronicus*, is set in a precisely imagined, if entirely unhistorical, ancient Roman world. Its lack of a specific historical source or context has led many scholars to sideline this early work in favour of the more canonical 'Roman Plays', *Julius Caesar*, *Antony and Cleopatra*, and *Coriolanus*.[2] The first two of these have had an especially palpable influence on popular cinema.[3] Despite its lack of historical specificity, *Titus Andronicus* has been judged to be 'an important engagement with Rome and the Romans',[4] and even 'a more characteristic piece of Roman history than the three great plays of Shakespeare which are generally grouped under that name'.[5]

Rome, according to some critics, just happens to be the setting for the revenge play *Titus Andronicus*. That is a criticism that can also be levelled at any number of historical dramas, including *The Robe*, *Quo Vadis*, or *The Fall of the Roman Empire*. Another criticism, also not unlike the ridicule heaped on historical dramas by some historians, is that the world of *Titus Andronicus* is an unrecognisable mixture of Roman politics and history: 'it includes all the political institutions that Rome ever had. The author seems anxious, not to get it all right, but to get it all in'.[6]

It is true that the play is, as Charles and Michelle Martindale put it, 'an ostentatiously classical play'.[7] It makes visible reference to classical texts, including the use of the works of Ovid to precipitate the discovery of the criminals Chiron and Demetrius, and allusions to the rape of Lucretia and the killing of Verginia from the early books of Livy, as well as frequent reference to Troy and the *Aeneid*. There is a significant amount of Latin spoken or quoted in the play (and in the film too). There are references to Roman customs and religion throughout, and it has been pointed out that the city is named more frequently here than in *Julius Caesar* and *Antony and Cleopatra* combined.[8] All this, together with frequent mentions of specific places in the city (the Capitol, the Senate, the Pantheon), adds up to a heightened sense of 'authenticity'.

Titus Andronicus' most noteworthy feature, for the purposes of this study, is the intense focus on the city of Rome, its institutions, and its values, not at a specific time, but throughout its history. In this first dramatic exploration of Rome, Shakespeare creates a world in which starkly primitive republican virtue and imperial decadence coexist and compete—it is a kind of reflection or dissertation on the different ways of 'being Roman'. In the film

Titus, director Julie Taymor's Rome is entirely anachronistic, but it looks back to Shakespeare's own anachronisms.[9] Taking her lead from this feature of the play Taymor merely extends its anachronism through her striking use of archaeological sites and through reference to fascist Rome and to contemporary culture. In addition, the play's extravagantly violent spectacles—often viewed as a structural and stylistic weakness—can be seen as a demonstration of the collapse of virtue in the face of corruption and decadence. That is certainly Julie Taymor's interpretation of the role of spectacle in the play and in her film. We will see that evidence for this can be found in the focus on the amphitheatre at the beginning and end of the film, and in the so-called 'Penny Arcade Nightmares', set pieces that are specifically focused on negotiating the brutal events at the heart of the drama.

Shakespeare's Rome and cinematic Rome

The extraordinary vividness, persuasiveness, and verisimilitude of Shakespeare's Rome are often noted. The plays may not give us '"true" pictures of the ancient world', as Michelle and Charles Martindale say, but they do give 'a sense of a possible past culture with its own imaginative consistency'.[10] The question of the 'truth' of history, the Martindales remind us, is in any case rather complicated once we have accepted the blurring of the lines between fiction and history. This is as true of Shakespeare's Rome as it is of the Rome of historical epic films; historian, dramatist, and filmmaker all take part, as we have seen throughout this book, in the telling of stories about the past. The plays with which Shakespeare brings ancient Rome to life are perhaps the beginning of the tradition of such story-telling in historical films. While *Titus* does not market or conceive of itself as a historical drama, it does have some associations with that genre, not least because Shakespeare's Rome (albeit from his more 'mainstream' plays, *Julius Caesar* and *Antony and Cleopatra*) is a key ingredient in many Roman historical films.

Of course, Elizabethan England's perception of and interest in the Roman world differed markedly from our own, and from that of the Hollywood epics. But one of the most dominant themes we see in films set in ancient Rome is the conflict between Rome's republican and idealised past and its ultimate degeneration into corruption and tyranny. This theme is central to *Julius Caesar*, underlies much of what is said in *Antony and Cleopatra*, and informs both *Titus Andronicus* and *Coriolanus*. Furthermore, the focus on the city of Rome itself and its physical landmarks (for example the Capitol and the city walls), which is such a characteristic feature of all the Roman plays, is evidently part of the tradition of cinematic Rome. What Shakespeare evokes with words in the Elizabethan theatre, the cinema reconstructs in elaborate sets, in which features such as the Senate or the Colosseum suggest the presence of antiquity. In the plays Rome often functions as a symbol or metaphor for power itself. This is another popular feature in historical films: for instance Crassus' speech in *Spartacus* about the need to abase oneself before Rome, Messala's fascination with Rome's power at the beginning of *Ben-Hur*, or Maximus' 'Rome is the light' speech at the start of *Gladiator*.

Although I would not go as far as to say, as David Fredrick does, that 'the constitutive visual dialogue of *Titus* is first and foremost with Roman movie epics', it is true that there are numerous visual and stylistic points of contact between it and some major epic productions (for example *The Robe* or *Sign of the Cross* (1932)).[11] In addition, the central conflict between Titus and Saturninus, which embodies the two different 'myths' of Rome—stark morality against lavish decadence—lets *Titus* tap straight into the cinematic history of Rome. Like *Gladiator*, *Titus* is the story of a Roman general's struggle to exact vengeance on an overwhelming autocrat who is characterised by an infantile love of luxury and by excessive, and possibly misguided, libido.[12] Arguably, Shakespeare's Saturninus is a model or archetype for the volatile tyrants we meet in *Quo Vadis*, *The Robe*, and *The Fall of the Roman Empire*. Certainly, the ostentation of Saturninus' surroundings (for instance the orgy or the elaborate throne in the Senate room) in *Titus* owes a great deal to those earlier cinematic emperors. Again, Fredrick may be right when he claims that 'with its orgies, bathing, and amphitheater scenes, *Titus* engages a central thematic concern of the classic Hollywood films'.[13] The fascination with Roman decadence and excess that underlies so many of the big Hollywood productions of the 1930s, 1940s, and 1950s certainly reverberates in parts of this film.

The stylistic concept: 'metahistory'

Titus has been described as 'a quintessentially postmodern adaptation: playful, self-conscious, heterogeneous'.[14] It breaks down the conventions of traditional realistic cinema and introduces theatrical distancing devices to create an idiosyncratic visual style. As a result of Taymor's approach, *Titus* is a complete departure from the conventions of historical film. It challenges the viewer to draw parallels between past and present, at times to question whether the past is really as distant as we might like it to be. Visually, the film is typified by the strikingly anachronistic production design, which is entirely in keeping with what we know about Shakespeare's own use of anachronism both in this and in other plays.[15] This runs counter to the conventions of verisimilitude, if not always authenticity, that govern the other historical dramas we have examined. To the anachronism we can add Taymor's interest in oscillating deliberately and consciously between realism and artifice in her use of cinematic technique. She says this of her stylistic concept for the film: 'Though I was committed to creating a film whose world would be grounded in a sense of possibility and reality, I was also committed to the ideas I had formulated in the theatre that juxtaposed stylized and naturalistic imagery'.[16] This commitment to a concept of cinema as a 'magical tool' that can be used, as Taymor puts it, 'to bend time and perspective, to alter our perceptions of the familiar to the point where we give our audience a totally fresh view of the subject',[17] has implications for her representation of the past on the screen.

Taymor's real achievement, supported by the production designer Dante Ferretti (associated with a number of Fellini's and Pasolini's films) is in making the city of Rome itself the protagonist of the film, especially through her use of locations. Much of the filming took place on archaeological sites (such as at Hadrian's Villa, and at the Archaeological Park around the Via Appia Antica), and at E.U.R., the intended site of the Esposizione Universale Roma (the world exhibition planned for 1942 that never took place), a showcase for Mussolini's grandest architectural plans. By juxtaposing ancient Rome with its fascist re-interpretations, Taymor creates not a film about ancient Rome, but a film about how ancient Rome resonates through history and today. *Titus* is, as Jonathan Bate says in his introduction to the screenplay, 'a meditation on history', or a 'metahistory'.[18] This term is often used with reference to the films of Pasolini to describe their focus on the continuity between ancient myth and modern society, and similarities between Taymor and Pasolini have often been noted. Fellini, however, is perhaps a more obvious point of reference for Taymor—she certainly names him more frequently in connection with *Titus* than she does Pasolini. All three of Fellini's Roman films, *La Dolce Vita*, *Fellini Satyricon*, and *Roma* are important presences in the visual style of *Titus*, and in its interpretation of the city of Rome. The exuberance and decadence of *La Dolce Vita* is clearly a significant influence on the characterisation and appearance of Saturninus and his court, especially in the partying scenes. *Satyricon* is echoed in the emphasis on corruption and decadence, in the use of landscape as metaphor, in some of the costuming (for example Tamora's headdress, the soldiers' armour). Despite the visual allusions, there are also significant differences between *Titus* and *Satyricon*. While Fellini emphasises the distance and inaccessibility of the past, in *Titus* the past is not remote at all; it seeps into the present through the locations and through the use of Shakespeare's words by living, breathing actors. Where *Satyricon* was about a far away planet where people did things very differently, and which was created entirely in the director's imagination and in the studio, *Titus* is about a world in which past and present continually brush up against one another, much as they do in the city of Rome itself.

In this emphasis on the simultaneity of past and present in Rome, *Titus* is closest to Fellini's final treatment of Rome, *Roma*, a depiction of Rome's most celebrated feature, the coexistence of its many different epochs, most famously described by Sigmund Freud:

> Now, let us make the fantastic assumption that Rome is not a place where people live, but a psychical entity with a similarly long, rich past, in which nothing that ever took shape has passed away and all previous phases of development exist beside the most recent.[19]

Taymor's Rome: the Square Colosseum; the she-wolf

Although she mistakenly believes that E.U.R was 'Mussolini's government centre', the use Taymor makes of this setting, which she says 'perfectly embodied the concept of the film', is illuminating.[20] The Palazzo della Civiltà Italiana (known as the Square Colosseum) built by Mussolini's chief architect, Marcello Piacentini, is intended to be a meeting of classical monumentality with functional modernism, and it has come to stand as an emblem for Mussolini's architectural plans, and for the fascist utopia of E.U.R. For Taymor's purposes, the way in which it evokes the continuity between the ancient Roman Empire and its fascist recreation is ideal. Its first appearance in *Titus* is as the setting for the leadership contest between Bassianus and Saturninus that is the start of the play itself. Shakespeare's text envisages the setting for the contest and for the beginning of the play as the Capitol, the summit of the Capitoline hill, and symbolic centre of Rome. In Taymor's version this beginning and Titus' entry and speech have been reversed, and the Capitol as the heart of Rome has been displaced by the use of the Colosseum as the site of Titus's entry. In the leadership contest the Capitol is replaced again by the Square Colosseum—a radical change of both time and place. The fact that the director believes E.U.R. to be Mussolini's government centre makes this change still more relevant for her. The old republican associations of the Capitoline hill are discarded for the new imperial monolith, an echo of the Flavian amphitheatre with its associations of monumentality and power, as well as decadence and corruption. The building takes up the entire frame when it is first seen as the camera travels down its length to the monumental front steps on which young Lucius is sitting and then up again as the black flags of mourning are dropped down from the many arches that are intended to mirror those of the Colosseum. The camera angle of shooting the building from the steps below to underline its towering monumentality is repeated and also emphasised by the musical score.

During this scene outside the Square Colosseum, as we have emerged from the darkness of the amphitheatre and the mausoleum into the bright sunshine, the film's exuberant anachronism really comes to life. Young Lucius is seen reading the *Roman Times*, just before Bassianus and Saturninus and their cronies begin to crowd into the piazza, Saturninus in a 1930s convertible car, covered with bullet-proof glass, Bassianus in a 1950s convertible. The motorcades are led by soldiers on horseback and Titus later arrives in a chariot drawn by four horses. The music is jazzy, in a style reminiscent of the 1930s. Marcus Andronicus is dressed in a white suit, over which a toga-type cloth with a deep red border is draped. He speaks into a microphone adorned with the logo 'SPQR News'. For the time being, all this seems fairly harmless: the antagonism between the parties is reasonably controlled, and the comedic touches (the paper, the microphone, the football team flags used for the two factions) keep the atmosphere quite light, especially by contrast with the previous scenes in the amphitheatre and in the mausoleum. The moment that Saturninus is crowned, however, we encounter a rather different—more threateningly archaic—face to Rome. With an abrupt cut following the placing of the laurel wreath on Saturninus' head, we find ourselves looking into the eyes of the rather savage version of the Roman she-wolf, its jaws wide open. This turns out to be a huge bronze head placed over Saturninus' throne; it is a ferocious animal, in Julie Taymor's own words 'the mother of all human beings'. Saturninus is enthroned beneath the open jaws of this terrifying mythical she-wolf. The statue can be seen in the Capitoline Museum, but without the sideways view and the suckling children underneath, this symbol, just the head and the wide-open jaws, harnessed with a kind of muzzle, bears no hint of the nurturing aspect that goes hand in hand with the wolf's traditional Roman representation. The wolf's head over Saturninus' throne seems also to take the place of the imperial eagle that is so frequently associated with cinematic Rome—and often used as a way of drawing out the parallels with Nazi Germany. Taymor's film is devoid of eagles, but the savage aspect of the wolf symbol epitomises Taymor's interpretation of the play. This is reinforced a little later, when a close-up shot of panting dogs during Saturninus' hunt echoes the open-jawed wolf and drives home the dangers that emanate from this central symbol.

Taymor's Rome: new and old

Titus retains some of Shakespeare's ostentatious classicism in the many verbal and visual allusions to Roman antiquity. Thus Taymor has retained Titus' use of Verginius as a mythical example for his own murder of Lavinia, Lavinia's use of Ovid's *Metamorphoses*, and some Latin quotations too, despite the fact that all of these are not easy for a mainstream audience to appreciate or understand. To the verbal allusions to the ancient world Taymor adds visual touches such as the modified image of the she-wolf over Saturninus' throne in the Senate, the Greek vase-paintings that decorate the banqueting room, the toga-like scarves worn over the senators' suits and ties, and the still portrait of the bathers early on in the film. Moreover, the use of Roman archaeological sites (Hadrian's Villa, the Villa of the Quintilii and the arena in Pula) provides a visual equivalent to Shakespeare's classical allusions: these are not just reconstructed sets, but places that bear signs or traces of the past, and which allude through their own ruined state to the ruined classical past that underlies the play.

Cinecittà itself could not fail to exert its own mythic influence, and Taymor talks frequently about the presence of Fellini's set-makers there and mentions work they did for her film (such as the decoration for the banquet scene). But the city itself inspires her unique approach to the building of the Rome of *Titus*, and to visualising Shakespeare's own approach to the historical, or metahistorical, setting of his play. In her director's notes appended to the illustrated screenplay, Taymor describes her initial approach to the creation of her cinematic Rome:

> Modern Rome, built on the ruins of ancient Rome, offered the perfect stratification for the setting of the film. I wanted to blend and collide time, to create a singular period that juxtaposed elements of ancient barbaric ritual with familiar, contemporary attitude and style. Instead of re-creating Rome, 400 A.D., the locations of the film would include the ruins of Hadrian's villa, the baths of Caracalla, the Colosseum, etc., as they are today, with all their corroded beauty, centuries of graffiti and ghastly, ghostly history.[21]

In this interpretation, the ancient past is encountered as ruin rather than reconstruction: what is 'brought to life' is the process by which the past, slowly, has become the present. In theory, this approach is reminiscent of Fellini's idea of the filmmaker as archaeologist, piecing together fragments in order to create a world that is only a trace of an inaccessible, remote past. Taymor's extensive use of locations rather than studio sets makes an important difference. In this way, *Titus* becomes properly a film about Rome itself, not about a moment in its history, like *Quo Vadis* or *Spartacus*, and not about Rome as a tourist site, like

Roman Holiday (1953) or *Three Coins in the Fountain* (1954), but a film about the way in which past and present interact, collide, and are in constant dialogue with one another. Nowhere is this more striking than in the fascinating intercutting of two very different locations near the start of the film: the Palazzo della Civiltà Italiana and the remains of Hadrian's Villa. The contrast between the two locations is highlighted by having Titus and his family occupy the ruined villa, while Saturninus and Tamora celebrate their wedding in the palazzo.

Titus, a broken man associated with the virtues of the past that are no longer valued in the 'new' Rome of Saturninus, is surrounded by the evocative ruins of the site. In the DVD (special edition, released 2006) commentary, Taymor describes Titus as resembling a 'deteriorating bust', and a 'broken down sculpture'. She has had the set designers add a colossal hand and foot, the broken fragments of a statue, to the location in order to highlight the correspondence between Titus and his physical surroundings, and as an ironic foreshadowing of the further physical disintegration of the protagonist that is to follow (see Fig. 7). It is at this point in the film that the height of the palazzo (highlighted earlier, as we saw, with the camera angles from below it) gains in significance. It becomes clear now that occupation of this building means absolute power over Rome. The scene begins with Aaron overlooking the fine view of the city from one of the balconies of the palazzo—a panorama that already begins to suggest his power, and which will be developed shortly. Together with Tamora, Aaron is then seen looking down from the balcony and straight into the courtyard of Hadrian's Villa. This is a physical impossibility of course, which highlights their now secure position high up on the 'Capitoline', able to pursue power and influence through surveillance. Aaron and Tamora's position on the balcony is maintained even when we first see

Saturninus descending the steps from the palazzo into the villa; there are two shadowy figures high above, keeping everything in their sight, controlling both Titus and Saturninus. In the scene that follows, Tamora engineers a reconciliation of sorts between the emperor and Titus, which ends with Bassianus and Lavinia being invited to join the wedding party. As they, along with Saturninus, climb the steps away from Titus' crumbling ruins and up into Saturninus' modern realm, the film's action pauses for the first Penny Arcade Nightmare—a depiction of the depth of Tamora's resentment and grief at Titus' killing of her son—which alerts us to the violence that is simmering underneath Tamora's manipulation of Saturninus. When Tamora rejoins the party in the palazzo, Aaron's words elucidate what has just happened:

7   *Titus at Hadrian's Villa*
with statue fragments
added by set designers.
Image: British Film Institute.
Copyright: Buena Vista/
Disney Corporation.

Tamora is triumphant and safe for now. Aaron himself finds his power over Rome ascending too as he watches the dawn rise over the city, another panoramic view that drives home the control Aaron is now able, via Tamora, to exercise.

To conclude, the juxtaposition of the ruins of Hadrian's Villa with the Square Colosseum, and the emphasis on the height of the latter building and the views from it demonstrate how Taymor's approach to Shakespeare's Rome works as a novel cinematic interpretation of some old issues in films about Rome: the conflicts between virtuous individuals and a tyrannical state, the influence of powerful women over weak and corrupt emperors, and the contrast between Rome's crumbling republican past and its monumental, imperial present. The gleaming marble of the Palazzo della Civiltà Italiana with its arches and its monumental steps and statues is a distorted mirror image of the shining white marble set of, say, *The Fall of the Roman Empire*. Commodus' palace in *Gladiator* commands similar views of the dawn over the city, just at the point when Commodus' machinations reach their nadir; it is the image of surveillance and power associated with Rome's cinematic tyrants at least since *Quo Vadis* has Nero looking over the burning city.

In a way, Saturninus can be said to be inhabiting the proper world of the cinematic Roman Empire. He has a banquet and an orgy and—although anachronistically dressed—he behaves and lives exactly as a bad emperor does in historical epic. Only the presence of the wolf in place of the eagle hints at the difference in this approach to Rome's power. On the other hand, Titus' insistence on archaic and ritualised behaviour is mirrored in his physical locations. The locations associated with Titus himself are the amphitheatre and the mausoleum (filmed at Hadrian's Villa, too), the crossroads at the Via Appia Antica (newly made by the set designers, but within the Archaeological Park, and within sight of the ruins that are there), and the Villa of the Quintilii in the Archaeological Park that forms the set for some of the scenes at Titus' home. All these locations resonate with authenticity and bring antiquity properly into the film's representation of Rome: they bear the real traces of history, they are actual fragments of the past, and are clearly differentiated from Saturninus' domain. Saturninus' association with fascist Rome, combined with his bombastic, excessive style, marks him clearly as an enemy of republican virtue and a fully subscribed tyrant in the mould of Nero or Caligula.

In a manner that is frequently reminiscent of Fellini's *Roma*, Taymor highlights the coexistence of past and present, the visibility of cultural and collective memories in the very fabric of the city. What Taymor's cinematography and direction are telling us is that there is no such thing as history or the past, that to attempt to isolate and interpret historical events, or to present them realistically and objectively on the screen is not a viable project. Of course, the juxtaposition of past and present in the use of locations and in costuming is staged and artificial—the very things that mainstream historical drama tries to avoid. But the distance provided by this artifice helps the film to portray the right uncertainty. We are never, in this film, allowed to wallow in the illusion that we are looking at the past through a window, despite the fact that of all the films we have examined this is the one that makes the most extensive use of real historical locations. In the use of these 'layers' of Rome, as she put it, Taymor has created a film that represents history itself, and shows how a film can represent the past as open-ended, as a challenge to the present instead of simply the story of individual struggles set against a 'historical' background.

A 'theatre of cruelty': Colosseum and penny arcade

From its earliest performances, *Titus Andronicus* was criticised as being all spectacle at the expense of a decent plot. In effect, this is what attracted Taymor to the play in the first instance. The theme of violence as entertainment is at the heart of her interpretation; it has also led her to make the interesting directorial decisions between realism and stylisation. We turn now to two of the most striking inventions in *Titus*, both in a way answers to the play's fascination with spectacular violence: the framing device of the Roman amphitheatre, and the so-called Penny Arcade Nightmares.

Titus is based on Julie Taymor's theatrical production of *Titus Andronicus*, staged in New York in 1994. On the stage the oscillation we have already mentioned between realism and stylisation was highlighted by a giant gold proscenium arch and red curtains that framed the action throughout: a fairly explicit way of saying to an audience that 'this is theatre, not real life'.[22] In the film, this device is replaced by the introduction of the Roman arena as the 'theatre' in which the events unfold and ultimately conclude. Taymor explains the analogy: 'For the film I chose an equivalent but more cinematic architectural structure to function in the same symbolic manner: the Roman Colosseum, the archetypal theater of cruelty, where violence as entertainment reached its apex.'[23]

For some viewers, the amphitheatre's circle will inevitably bring to mind not only Shakespeare's theatre, but also (perhaps primarily) the tradition of cinematic Rome and its violent spectacles, and thus the analogy between the Roman spectators at the gladiatorial games and the spectators in the modern cinema.[24] Once more, then, we see the Colosseum brought into the centre of a vision of ancient Rome and used to draw explicit parallels between ancient and modern decadence. In drawing these parallels, Taymor focuses especially on the experience of the spectator, as Elsie Walker recognises: 'for Taymor, *Titus* is as much about violence as about how we experience violence as entertainment. In a world where the media and movies present a desensitized view of violence, Taymor wishes to reinstall a sense of shock at violence.'[25]

The film does not begin in Rome, ancient or modern, but in the kitchen of a city apartment 'in Brooklyn or Sarajevo', where a young boy is playing furiously with toy soldiers—Roman, twentieth-century, and supernatural—to the sound of cartoons blaring from the television. This scene is how the action of *Titus* comes to life: the child's play enacting the 'barbaric ritual' of warfare results in an explosion; the child hides under the table, and the last soldiers standing on the table are two Roman legionaries in red cloaks. For Taymor, this prologue 'encapsulates the spectrum of "violence" as it transforms, in a matter of seconds, from innocuous entertainment to horrific reality'.[26] The boy is lifted away from the kitchen by a clown or strongman wearing a First World War leather helmet, and he transports the child into the middle of a Roman amphitheatre. Here, the clown holds the child aloft like a trophy in the arena to the sound of cheering from an invisible crowd.

We get a first intimation of the interplay of past and present: in the well-preserved remains of the Roman arena in Pula, the 'ghosts of past centuries [are] being awakened',[27] it is their voices we hear cheering. The camera circles around the man and the child as the clown himself turns in a circle to show the saved child off to the spectators who are not there, and to show off the circle of the arena to the spectator in the cinema. Ridley Scott does the same thing with his computer-generated Colosseum. In the middle of the arena we see the house that the boy was rescued from, ablaze; The house has also become part of the spectacle performed for the ghostly crowds, and for the cinema audience, who stand in for the absent spectators.[28]

The child picks up a dusty action figure of a Roman soldier from the ground, and in an instant an army of 'real' soldiers, dressed exactly like the toy figure, begin to advance into the arena. The first thing one notices about this procession is that all the soldiers are caked in a thick layer of clay or mud, perhaps as though they had just been excavated, and in their weird formations the marching troops look most like the Chinese terracotta army, suggesting a funeral rather than a triumph. The entry of this strange troop is choreographed so that they move like mechanical figures, a kind of caricature of the many Riefenstahl-style triumphal marches in other history films. In fact, this choreographed movement could be seen as highlighting the robotic, menacing quality of the Roman army, in a manner that is reminiscent of how Stanley Kubrick showed the Roman troops moving against the slave army in the centre-piece battle scene in *Spartacus*. (In *Spartacus*, the Roman troops are played by Spanish soldiers, in *Titus* they are members of the Croatian police force.) As Walker points out, this choreographed way of moving constitutes 'part of a picture of Rome as rigid, ceremonial, politically prescriptive, a facade of order'.[29]

As in a proper Roman triumph, we see prisoners paraded in humiliation, the booty displayed to follow the victorious general in his chariot. The motorbikes and the tanks, the barbed wire and Plexiglas are a clear first indication of the kind of world we are looking at in this film. This may be ancient Rome, but there will be no red and gold soldiers here, no white marble, and no screaming crowds of extras. The triumph has become, in the silent arena, a mockery of the spectacles we expect in the cinema. Titus' first speech appears to equate the arena with Rome, as he addresses the empty seats with the words 'Hail, Rome'. The camera circles around him, drawing attention to the circle of the arena that suggests also the circular enclosure of the Elizabethan theatre that is the stage, and the world, of the play.

In the scene that follows immediately on Titus' entrance into Rome/the arena, we are at a Roman bath, a set constructed at Cinecittà. This is the moment when, according to the director, 'the film moves into a mode of reality', when the clay is washed off the soldiers, who at the start of the shot are posing immobile, like ancient statues. The missing limbs of two of the figures accentuate the allusion to ancient sculpture, to the fragmented way in which antiquity survives into the present. But 'as the clay streams off the bodies of the soldiers, revealing their skin, the actors transform from mythic sculptures to human beings',[30] and so the juxtaposition of artifice and realism that characterises this film is established.

We turn now to the second meta-cinematic device, the Penny Arcade Nightmares, also a concept developed on the basis of the stage version, with the purpose of offering distance from and a space for reflection on the extreme violence depicted in the film. Here Taymor describes how these episodes functioned in the play on stage:

> I devised the concept of the 'Penny Arcade Nightmares' (PANs) to portray the inner landscapes of the mind as affected by external actions. These stylized, haikulike images appeared at various points throughout the play, counterpointing the realistic events in a dreamlike, surreal, and mythic manner ... These tableaux vivants were contained in floating gold frames and revealed by the drawing of tattered red velvet curtains. The images were further abstracted by their being positioned behind a translucent layer of plastic that was scarred with

scratches and spattered and smudged with black ink, like
a rotting old photograph.[31]

Intended to mirror the stage itself, these miniature dramas
within the drama highlighted the artifice involved in any theatrical
production. But the horror of what was depicted within the gold
frame and curtains was so devoid of pleasure as to force the
audience to question the notion of violence as entertainment.[32]
In the film, the PANs, which are visually reminiscent of music
videos at times, reflect the ways in which realistic cinema exploits
and makes aesthetic violence as entertainment. In this way, the
PANs form a part of Taymor's exploration of the representation
of violence and horror and of an audience's experience of this.

The first two PANs are clearly delineated and self-enclosed
sequences in which characters' thoughts or imagination are
projected in a miniature film within the film. After this point, the
limits of reality and illusion begin to be eroded. The third PAN
occurs during Lavinia's revelation of the names of her torturers.
The sequence depicts the violence done to her through a series
of visual metaphors that are feverishly intercut with Lavinia's
reading of the Philomela episode in Ovid's *Metamorphoses*, and
her writing out of the rapists' names in the sand, clutching
Marcus' stick between her stumps.

The two subsequent PANs further blur the boundaries between
the real and the imaginary: first in the strange episode in which
the heads of the sons of Titus and his own amputated hand are
presented in a kind of circus van while Marcus, young Lucius,
Lavinia, and Titus look on at this play within the film that tests
the limits of our (and Titus') endurance of the spectacular horrors
of this plot. The reappearance here of the clown who had brought
young Lucius into the arena at the start of the film reveals this
moment as a turning point. As Taymor puts it 'nightmares are

now reality and madness can be confused with sanity'.[33] Titus' shocking reaction to the scene is to laugh—in this he pre-empts the audience's own horrified laughter and provides yet another opportunity to reflect on what would be an appropriate reaction to such cruelty framed as entertainment. Continuing with the exploration of the boundaries between illusion and reality, the final PAN, Tamora's production of 'Rape, Murder, and Revenge', begins by appearing to be a figment of Titus' crazed imagination. Soon, however, it becomes clear that this is no vision, but a nightmare staged with the intention of making Titus believe he has gone mad. The purpose of the PANs—to highlight and to disrupt the boundaries between reality and artifice, and to drive home the trauma of the violence that punctuates the play— reaches its climax when the film returns us, after the massacre at Titus' dinner party, with a jolt into the arena. When the frantic slaughter concludes with Lucius aiming his gun at Saturninus the camera pulls back to reveal the scene of Titus' catastrophic dinner party in the centre of the arena: a spectacle of excessive and theatrical violence. Reality and play have merged and become one, in a gesture that clearly mirrors the opening of the film. 'The nightmare takes over the plot', as Taymor describes this moment of revelation that the arena is all there is, and that we, finally, have been sitting in the seats all along watching silently.[34]

We/they continue to watch in silence the aftermath of the massacre, when Marcus assumes control of the situation while the clown appears once again and begins to cover the bodies with clear plastic sheeting. *Titus Andronicus* concludes with the restoration of order to the city, the punishment of the famously unrepentant Aaron, Lucius' final assumption of the throne, and mourning for Titus, who is conveyed, along with Lavinia to the tomb of the Andronici where the play had opened with the burial of the sons of Titus. By placing all this in the arena, under the silent gaze of the impassive spectators, it appears that Taymor's interpretation questions the validity of this healing process. It seems that these final acts are nothing but a continuation of a never-ending cycle of violence, that Rome is forever condemned to perform the spectacles of the arena. The image of Aaron, buried alive, but also somehow crucified creates an 'obvious visual parallel' with the crucified Kirk Douglas at the end of *Spartacus*, as David Fredrick sees it.[35] This cannot but evoke the mainstream Roman epic movie tradition of martyred Christians and slaves in the arena.

The end of *Titus*: salvation after all?

Taymor does not leave us with no hope of escape from the arena of endless violence. Instead, she gives us the experience and perspective of young Lucius, who has been present as an observer throughout and is now ready to come to the foreground. Young Lucius takes Aaron's baby out of the cage in which he has been imprisoned and begins to walk out of the arena. This is how the director describes the scene: 'As he walks, the infinite night sky within that single archway slowly gives way to dawn. The boy keeps moving towards the exit, towards the promise of daylight as if redemption were a possibility'.[36]

Critics have mixed feelings about this surprising ending. David McCandless, for example, can see that when he leaves the arena 'Young Lucius breaks the cycle of violence', but he is also critical of the final image as 'staging a wish-fulfilment fantasy, a dénouement uncomfortably comparable to a Hollywood Happy Ending'.[37] Elsewhere it is argued that Lucius 'walks with the baby out of the arena into the sunrise much as the boy Eliot carried the alien E.T. when they rode together on a bike off into the sky in Spielberg's *E.T.*'[38] That analogy is rather unconvincing; there are some more specific parallels to be drawn.

We have observed already a pattern of endings in Roman films that involves the protagonists turning their backs, physically or metaphorically, on Rome and its depravity. I would argue that in *Titus*, too, it seems that the future must belong to those who leave Rome behind. Varinia and her baby leave behind Rome and the crucified Spartacus; Livius and Lucilla walk away from the corrupt senators in the forum, Judah Ben-Hur retreats from Rome into domesticity and perhaps Christianity; Maximus finds refuge in Elysium; even Encolpio wanders away from the vile cannibalistic Roman nobles. So Lucius carries the baby Aaron away from the stricken Romans in their cruel arena towards a better future. Taymor's notes tell us that this possible redemption serves as a 'counterpoint to Shakespeare's dark tale of vengeance'. It seems finally that there can be no Roman story that does not include the fall of Rome and the rise of something better.

CONCLUSION

A t the end of this study of the cinematic stories and spectacles of ancient Rome what conclusions can we draw from the very different films we have examined? We began by looking at three films that are often considered to define the genre, only to discover that each of them in fact works to differentiate itself from a—perhaps quite mythical—generic Roman spectacle. William Wyler, Stanley Kubrick, and Anthony Mann all saw themselves as making a new kind of epic, just as Ridley Scott did a quarter of a century later. These directors were aware of the danger of overwhelming story with spectacle. Bringing the past to life, especially when that past is ancient Rome with its lavish banquets, extravagant games and shows, overwhelming triumphal processions, and decadent aristocrats with luxurious lifestyles always risks over-indulging in grandeur and splendour and ending up as 'wantonly expansive, hyperbolic, even hysterical' spectacle.[1]

In *Ben-Hur*, *The Fall of the Roman Empire* and *Gladiator* there are lavish triumphs, palaces, circuses, and so on, and it is easy to say that these spectacular aspects are what we watch the movies for. But the underlying narratives ensure that spectacle itself becomes a pivot in these films, as the central conflicts always revolve around subjects such as the opposition between republicanism and tyranny or the problems of oppression and imperialism, which invite reflection on the role of spectacle.

Tyranny is exemplified by spectacles such as the triumph or the arena, Roman decadence declares itself in displays of splendour, and slavery is seen as the reduction of human beings to objects of the powerful and humiliating gaze of Rome. Thus every film about Rome becomes a film about spectacle.

Spartacus stands out from the rest of the mainstream examples as a more visually austere movie and arguably the one that is most obviously aware of the problems associated with letting the spectacular aspects of Roman decadence overwhelm the story. But we saw that Wyler and Mann, and later Scott, also aimed to avoid the trap of over-indulgence in spectacle. More than that, we found that all four films demonstrate a keen awareness of the role of spectacle in ancient Rome, which has the effect of a critique. Wyler, for instance, gives us the chariot race, but also shows through Judah's path of conversion that such spectacular events are not the solutions they appear to be; Kubrick denies his audience the pleasure of a fight to the death between the two enemies and denounces Crassus' ultimate degeneracy by showing him to be capable only of looking, not of acting; Mann creates spectacles that are subverted by the absence of spectators or overpowered by the spectacle of nature or landscape. Scott's film has been criticised as being all form and no substance, and certainly it comes close to wallowing in visual pleasure for its own sake. But Scott ultimately avoids such criticism by creating in Maximus a protagonist who is himself contemptuous of the pleasure that others ('the mob') take in his spectacular performances. The shows in the arena become the protagonist's means of achieving his personal and political goals: death, and freedom from tyranny for Rome. By endowing the violence with such narrative significance *Gladiator* appears to be able to have its cake and eat it: to provide violence as entertainment and to criticise the society of spectacle that endorses this.

Through its pivotal role in the stories, spectacle provides both a commentary on itself and a strategy for identifying alternative stories. *Ben-Hur* and *Spartacus* both promised Christianity and personal freedom as the way out of this society of spectacle, while *Gladiator*, in true twenty-first-century style offered individualised spirituality and a retreat into the private sphere. *Fall* had no way out but to let history take its course, but the point about the futility of the spectacular was forcefully made nevertheless.

Having begun his career with Roberto Rossellini and the neorealists, and well known by the late 1960s as a highly idiosyncratic *auteur*, Fellini liked to poke fun at Hollywood's weakness for illusion, realism, strongly motivated characters and stories, and impressive spectacle. He was keenly aware of the Roman historical movie's tendency to let spectacle overwhelm story and decided to make this the concept of his film. In *Fellini Satyricon* he portrayed a society in which everything is spectacle—from torture to dinner to sex, there is nothing that is not performance. *Satyricon* severs the conventional link between spectacle and pleasure that dominates mainstream cinema. Instead of attracting the viewer to the world of the film, in Fellini spectacle is revolting and alienating. In this way, Rome is entirely defamiliarised—no longer a place of lavish luxury and appealing decadence, but a derelict, corrupt, empty shell of spectacle bereft of content or story.

With *Titus*, Julie Taymor returned to one of the oldest Roman historical fictions and to the beginnings of our fascination with the story and the spectacle of Rome. Against the background of late twentieth-century Hollywood's penchant for furiously violent and spectacle-ridden blockbusters and the rise of extreme brutality in videogames, Taymor turns to the original paradigm of violence as entertainment. Her invention of the Colosseum

device to frame Shakespeare's Roman revenge tragedy brings
to a head the issue of the audience's enjoyment of violence as
spectacle and shows how, finally, no story about ancient Rome
is free from this symbol of Roman excess. Where the arena is
avoided, as in *Spartacus* or *Fall*, its absence haunts the film
perhaps more than its presence would. In *Gladiator*, by contrast,
the Colosseum dominates the film as an emblem of Rome itself.
Fellini decided not to include it in *Satyricon* but its presence in
the preparatory thought and in Fellini's comments is enough to
convince us that here, too, the amphitheatre stands for Rome
in a sense. By replacing the theatre with the arena and adopting
Fellini's approach to Rome as a city of layers in which past and
present coexist Taymor forges in *Titus* a knowing commentary
on the traditions of cinematic Rome. The film also makes a fitting
end to this study. Through visual allusions to earlier Roman epic
films and to Fellini's images of Rome *Titus* travels across the
spectrum of Roman spectacle and story. The image of the arena
bookends this time-travelling film and reminds viewers that,
whatever the story, spectacle is never far from Rome.

NOTES

Introduction

1 Michael Wood, *America in the Movies: Or, 'Santa Maria, It Had Slipped my Mind'* (London, 1975), p. 184.

2 The term 'visual pleasure' is associated with Laura Mulvey's influential essay 'Visual Pleasure and Narrative Cinema' first published in *Screen* 16.3 (1975), pp. 6–18. Mulvey revolutionised film studies with her polemical analysis of the sexual imbalance that predominates in classical Hollywood cinema. Her focus was especially on the ways in which visual pleasure is associated with a male spectator's power over a female object of the gaze. Her position is best summed up in one of the essay's section headings: 'Woman as image/man as bearer of the look'.

3 David Eldridge has written in some detail about the role of the historical researcher in Hollywood in *Hollywood's History Films* (London, 2006), pp. 127–51.

4 Robert Rosenstone, 'History in Images/History in Words', *American Historical Review* 93.5 (1988), pp. 1173–85, p. 1177.

5 André Bazin, 'The Myth of Total Cinema' (1946), republished in English in André Bazin, *What is Cinema?* trans. Hugh Gray (Berkeley, 1967; new edition, 2004), p. 22.

6 See Kristin Thompson, *Storytelling in the New Hollywood: Understanding Classical Narrative Technique* (Cambridge, MA, 1999), pp. 354–62.

Chapter 1: Narrative and spectacle, realism and illusion, and the historical film

1 Siegfried Kracauer, *Theory of Film: The Redemption of Physical Reality* (London, 1960), p. ix.

2 Ibid., p. 44.

3 Rudolf Arnheim, *Film as Art* (Berkeley, 1957), p. 133.

4 Robert Rosenstone, *History on Film/Film on History* (Harlow, 2006) is very good on Eisenstein as historian.

5 This theoretical outline is more fully treated in Anthony Easthope, 'Classic Film Theory and Semiotics', in J. Hill and P. Church Gibson (eds), *Film Studies: Critical Approaches* (Oxford, 2000), pp. 49–55.

6 See the seminal article (although not an easy read) by Colin MacCabe, 'Realism and the Cinema: Notes on Some Brechtian Theses', *Screen* 15.2 (1974), pp. 7–27.

7 See Mulvey 1975.

8 David Bordwell, *The Way Hollywood Tells It* (Berkeley and Los Angeles, 2006), p 118

9 David Bordwell, 'The Art Cinema as a Mode of Film Practice', in L. Braudy and M. Cohen (eds), *Film Theory and Criticism* (6th edition, Oxford, 2004), pp. 774–82, p. 779 (first published in *Film Criticism* 4.1 (1979), pp. 56–64).

10 Bordwell 2006, p. 180.

11 Ibid., p. 188.

12 Hayden White, *The Content of the Form* (Baltimore, 1987), p. 5.

13 Maria Wyke, *Projecting the Past: Ancient Rome, Cinema, and History* (London, 1997), p. 8–9.

14 White 1987, p. 1.

15 Ibid., p. 2.

16 Bordwell 2006, p. 28.

17 Quoted in David Bordwell, Janet Staiger and Kristin Thompson (eds), *The Classical Hollywood Cinema: Film Style and Mode of Production to 1960* (New York, 1985), p. 18.

18 Rosenstone 2006, pp. 47–8.

19 Bordwell, Staiger and Thompson 1985, p. 13.

20 See Rosenstone 2006, pp. 15–19, 50–5, and 163 on the differences between 'mainstream' and 'innovative' history films.

21 André Bazin, 'Will CinemaScope Save the Film Industry?', trans. Bert Cardullo, *Film Philosophy* 6.2 (2002), at http://www.film-philosophy.com/vol6-2002/n2bazin (originally published as 'Cinémascope: sauvera-t-il le cinéma? in *Esprit* 21.207–8 (October–November 1953), pp. 672–83).

22 Charles Barr, 'Cinemascope: Before and After', *Film Quarterly* 16.4 (summer 1963), pp. 4–24, p. 18.

23 First published in *Les lettres nouvelles*, February 1954; this translation by Johnathan Rosenbaum published online at http://lowres.uno.edu/classes/cyberlit/barthes01.htm#cine.

24 Ibid.

25 See Roland Barthes, *Roland Barthes by Roland Barthes*, trans. Richard Howard (Berkeley and Los Angeles, 1994), pp. 84–5, where he talks about walking through St Sulpice: 'the silliest of spectacles: ceremonial, religious, conjugal, and petit bourgeois . . .'

26 John Belton, *Widescreen Cinema* (Cambridge, MA, 1992), p. 202; Vivian Sobchack, '"Surge and Splendor": A Phenomenology of the Hollywood Historical Epic', *Representations* 29 (1990), pp. 24–49.

27 Wyke 1997, pp. 24–33; Philip Rosen, *Change Mummified: Cinema, Historicity, Theory* (Minneapolis and London, 2001), pp. 184–99.

28 Steve Neale, *Genre* (Chippenham, 1980), p. 35.

29 Ibid., p. 34.

30 Steve Neale, *Genre and Hollywood* (London and New York, 2000), p. 85.

31 But Kristin Thompson says that this argument is rather overstated and generalised. See Thompson 1999, pp. 344–5. On the importance of good story-telling to the contemporary blockbuster see also Warren Buckland, 'A Close Encounter with Raiders of the Lost Ark: Notes on Narrative Aspects of the New Hollywood Blockbuster', in Steve Neale and Murray Smith (eds), *Contemporary Hollywood Cinema* (London, 1998), pp. 166–77.

32 Booklet published by Universal City Studios (1967) containing advertising, publicity and promotion materials aimed at distributors.

33 Bosley Crowther, 'A Blockbuster', review of *Ben-Hur*, *New York Times*, 19 November 1959.

34 Bosley Crowther, 'Romans versus Barbarians: Spectacle and Melees in "Fall of Empire"', *New York Times*, 27 March 1964.

35 See the commentary feature on the making of this episode, available in the DVD boxed set of Series 1.

36 See Richard Rushton, 'Narrative and Spectacle in *Gladiator*', *CineAction* 56 (2001), pp. 35–43.

Chapter 2: *Ben-Hur*: 'Tale of the Christ' or tale of Rome?

1 Bruce Babington and Peter William Evans, *Biblical Epics: Sacred Narrative in the Hollywood Cinema* (Manchester, 1993), p. 182.

2 Prologue, *Quo Vadis* (1951).

3   But see William Fitzgerald, 'Oppositions, Anxieties, and Ambiguities in the Toga Move', in Sandra Joshel, Margaret Malamud and Donald T. McGuire (eds), *Imperial Projections: Ancient Rome in Popular Culture* (Baltimore and London, 2001), pp. 23–49, p. 38–9, for a different interpretation of the image's function.

4   *The Story of the Making of Ben-Hur*, press-book, 1959.

5   Although at the time MGM referred to the process as Camera 65. 70mm projection such as Ultra Panavision 70 and its successor Super Panavision 70 became the norm for such 'blockbusters', according to Belton 1992, p. 179.

6   *The Story of the Making of Ben-Hur*.

7   Janet Maslin in the *New York Times*, 19 December 1997.

8   Neale 1980, p. 35.

9   Ibid.

10   Martin Winkler, 'The Roman Empire in American Cinema after 1945', *Classical Journal* 93.2 (1997), pp. 167–96, p. 168. This article is the central treatment of the topic.

11   See Leon Hunt, 'What are Big Boys Made of? *Spartacus, El Cid,* and the Male Epic', in Pat Kirkham and Janet Thumin (eds), *You Tarzan: Masculinity, Movies, and Men* (New York, 1993), pp. 65–83.

12   See Mulvey 1975 for the gaze as a manifestation of power.

13   On Wyler's anti-fascism, see Winkler 1997, pp. 185–6; see Winkler 1997, pp. 176–8 on the symbol of the eagle.

14   See Belton 1992, pp. 198–9 on horizontal composition.

Chapter 3: *Spartacus* and the politics of story-telling

1   Philip Strick and Penelope Houston, *Sight and Sound* 41.2 (spring 1972), pp. 62–6.

2   See Wyke 1997, pp. 63–72, for a discussion of the range of ways in which *Spartacus* could be interpreted in the light of the US political agenda in that era.

3   The definitive treatment of this issue is Ina Rae Hark, 'Animals or Romans: Looking at Masculinity in *Spartacus*', in Steven Cohan and Ina Rae Hark (eds), *Screening the Male: Exploring Masculinities in Hollywood Cinema* (London, 1993), pp. 151–72. See also Wyke 1997, p. 70.

4   On this aspect see Alison Futrell, 'Seeing Red: Spartacus as Domestic Economist', in Joshel, Malamud and McGuire 2001, pp. 77–118.

5   Eugene Archer, 'Hailed in Farewell: "Spartacus" Gets Praise of Pleased Director', *New York Times*, 2 October 1960.

6 Two-disc special edition DVD of fully restored feature, released 2004.

7 Prologue, *Spartacus* (1960).

8 Duncan Cooper's research on *Spartacus* is unsurpassed. Published first in the journal *Cineaste*, this work is available on the Stanley Kubrick website http://www.visual-memory.co.uk/, along with a lot of other useful bibliography. Cooper's work is now also available in revised and updated versions in the recent collection, Martin Winkler (ed.), *Spartacus: Film and History* (Oxford, 2007). For ease of reference all my quotes from Cooper's research into the script and editing are from the essays in Winkler 2007.

9 Quoted in Cooper 2007, p. 45.

10 See Wyke 1997, p. 35.

11 See Winkler 1997, p. 172, and Wyke 1997, p. 71 on how the prologue fits in with the American and Christian values found elsewhere in films about Rome.

12 The editing decisions that amounted to the construction of a story of defeat rather than triumph are discussed by Cooper in 'Who Killed the Legend of Spartacus? Production, Censorship, and Reconstruction of Stanley Kubrick's Epic Film', in Winkler 2007, pp. 14–55.

13 Cooper 2007, pp. 23–31.

14 Ibid., p. 40.

15 Wyke 1997, p. 71.

16 Quoted in Winkler 2007, p. 3.

17 See Thomas Allen Nelson, *Kubrick: Inside a Film Artist's Maze* (Bloomington, IN, 1982), p. 58.

18 On landscape in *Spartacus* see Futrell 2001, pp. 106–7.

19 See J.H. Fenwick and J. Green-Armytage, 'Now You See It: Landscape and Anthony Mann', *Sight and Sound* 34.4 (1965), pp. 186–9; Jeanine Basinger, *Anthony Mann* (Middletown, CT, 2007), p. 50.

20 See for instance Mario Falsetto, *Stanley Kubrick: A Narrative and Stylistic Analysis* (Westport, CT, and London, 2001), p. 70.

21 See Hark 1993 on this.

22 See Archer 1960 and Stanley Kubrick, 'Words and Movies', *Sight and Sound* 30.1 (1961), p. 14.

23 See Futrell 2001 for a detailed discussion of this sequence.

24 Much of Trumbo's commentary on this is available in the scene-by-scene analysis included in the special edition DVD (2004).

25 See Nelson 1982, p. 58.

26 See also Futrell 2001, pp. 108–9.

27 See Cooper 2007, pp. 39–40.

28 See ibid., p. 39.

29 In the scene-by-scene analysis on the DVD special edition Trumbo rages against this 'vulgar throwback from another script'.

30 Hark 1993, p. 167.

31 But see Futrell 2001, pp. 109–10.

32 See Hark 1993, p. 168, which points out that Batiatus of all people is 'the only male left to occupy the driver's seat beside Varinia, usually reserved for the bearer of privileged masculinity, who will complete the heterosexual couple of classical Hollywood narrative closure'.

33 Stanley Kubrick, 'Notes on Film', *Observer Weekend Review*, 4 December 1960, p. 21.

34 Nelson 1982, p. 57.

35 For a detailed comparison between the *Spartacus* battle and the German battle in *Gladiator* see Geoff King, *New Hollywood Cinema: An Introduction* (New York, 2002), pp. 241–7.

36 Crassus' villa is the kind of lavish environment spectators expect for this sort of film. Some of the scenes at the villa were filmed at Hearst Castle in southern California, a kind of theme park of a house in which the millionaire Randolph Hearst had a Roman-style garden and pool built alongside a number of rooms decorated in the style of Pompeian villas. The use of this location as the home of the decadent millionaire Crassus has more than a little political poignancy.

37 See Winkler 1997, pp. 168–9 on these lines.

38 See Futrell 2001, pp. 108–9.

39 See ibid., pp. 106–7.

40 Bosley Crowther, '"Spartacus" Enters the Arena: Three-Hour Production Has Première at De Mille', *New York Times*, 7 October 1960.

Chapter 4: *The Fall of the Roman Empire*: The filmmaker as historian

1 Fenwick and Green-Armytage 1965, p. 187.

2 Martin Winkler, 'Cinema and the Fall of Rome', *Transactions of the American Philological Society* 125 (1995), pp. 135–54.

3 Ibid., p. 144.

4 Fenwick and Green-Armytage 1965, p. 187.

5 Antony Mann, 'Empire Demolition', *Films and Filming*, March 1964.

6 Christopher Wicking and Barrie Pattison, 'Interviews with Anthony Mann', *Screen* 10.4–5 (1969) , pp. 32–54.

7 Prologue, *The Fall of the Roman Empire* (1964).

8 Fenwick and Green-Armytage 1965, p. 189.

9 See Winkler 1995, p. 140.

10 See ibid., pp. 148–9, on the use of the she-wolf statue in the senate and on the old senator's speech.

11 Edward Gibbon, *The Decline and Fall of the Roman Empire* (London, 1998), p. 66.

12 Fenwick and Armytage-Green 1965, p. 187.

13 Basinger 2007, p. 162, says that Mann told an interviewer that the battle was not directed by him, and was not done as it should have been, because of a lack of funding by that stage in the process.

14 On the rhetoric of the architecture see Winkler 1995, p. 147, with references.

15 See also Winkler 1995, pp. 147–8.

16 Ibid., p. 144.

17 Fenwick and Armytage-Green 1965, p. 189.

18 See for example Peter Bondanella, *The Eternal City: Roman Images in the Modern World* (Chapel Hill, NC, 1987), pp. 224–5.

19 Pierre Sorlin, *The Film in History: Restaging the Past* (Oxford, 1980), pp. 110–11.

20 Wicking and Pattison 1969, p. 54.

21 Bosley Crowther, 'Romans versus Barbarians', *New York Times*, 27 March 1964.

Chapter 5: *Gladiator*: Making it new?

1 Douglas Bankston, 'Veni, Vidi, Vici', *American Cinematographer* 81.5 (2000), pp. 46–53.

2 See Bordwell 2006, pp. 129–34, on contemporary cinema's preference for the close-up.

3 David Thomson, 'The Riddler Has his Day', *Sight and Sound* 11.4 (2001), pp. 18–21, p. 21.

4 See Leslie Felperin, 'Decline and Brawl', *Sight and Sound* 10.6 (2000), p. 34, and Rushton 2001.

5 On the politics of the musical score see Arthur J. Pomeroy, 'The Vision of a Fascist Rome in *Gladiator*', in Martin Winkler (ed.), *Gladiator: Film and History* (Oxford, 2004), pp. 111–23, p. 121.

6 Prologue, *Gladiator* (2000).

7 For such an interpretation see for instance H. Muschamp, 'The Epic: Throwing Our Anxieties to the Lions', *New York Times*, 30 April 2000.

But Peter Rose may be right in diagnosing a 'virtual absence of any anxiety over empire'; see his essay, 'The Politics of *Gladiator*', in Winkler 2004, pp. 150–72; especially p. 156.

8 See Rosenstone 2006 on the conflict between history and the focus on individuals. See also Rose 2004, pp. 169–70, on this aspect of *Gladiator*.

9 See for instance Monica Cyrino, '*Gladiator* and Contemporary American Society', in Winkler 2004, pp. 124–49, p. 130.

10 See Parkes' recollections on the initial planning stages on the bonus feature 'The Tale of the Scribes' (part of the three-disc special edition released in 2005).

11 See Rose 2004, pp. 164–5, on Maximus' spirituality.

12 Doug Wick describes on the DVD bonus feature 'The Tale of the Scribes' how what they sold to Spielberg was 'a character journey, set in the Roman arena'.

13 Scott on the DVD (2005) commentary, referring to the script rewriting towards the end of the production. See Jon Solomon, '*Gladiator* from Screenplay to Screen', in Winkler 2004, pp. 1–15.

14 This also emerges from the conversation between Scott and Crowe on the DVD commentary. Again see Solomon 2004, pp. 12–13, on variant endings.

15 Fitzgerald 2001, p. 45.

16 See Natalie Zenon Davis, *Slaves on Screen* (Cambridge, MA, 2000), pp. 121–36, on *Amistad*.

17 Rose 2004, p. 163. See also Pomeroy 2004, p. 120.

18 See Pomeroy 2004, pp. 122–3, on the inherent political contradictions at the end of *Gladiator*. See Rosenstone 2006, pp. 16–17, on the 'progressive view of the past' that characterises most if not all history films.

19 See Rushton 2001, p. 43. Compare Maria Wyke, 'Film Style and Fascism: *Julius Caesar* (1953)', *Film Studies* 4 (2004), pp. 58–74, pp. 61–2, on the triumphal procession in *Julius Caesar* (1953).

20 The three-disc special edition DVD, released in 2005.

21 Although when Commodus is seen a little later, playing with a model Colosseum, images of both Mussolini's and Hitler's penchants for such models do seem to be deliberately evoked.

22 The 'petals' are actually Remembrance Day poppies, with the pins extracted. If one looks closely one can see the holes in the centres.

There is a weird, if unintentional, irony to this cavalier use of vast quantities of this very potent symbol.

23 See Douglas Bankston, 'Death or Glory', *American Cinematographer* 81.5 (2000), pp. 34–45, p. 44.

24 Ron Magid, 'Rebuilding Ancient Rome', *American Cinematographer* 81.5 (2000), pp. 54–9, p. 55.

25 Bordwell 2006, pp. 58–9. He quotes Ridley Scott, who calls this process 'layering'.

26 See Thomson 2001, p. 18: '"Beautifully photographed" is a term that merges characterless proficiency with the kind of buying eye that so undermines Ridley Scott as an artist'.

27 In Bankston 2000 Scott talks about his interest in 'worlds' that comes from his advertising background.

28 See Chapter 1 in this volume.

29 John Simon, 'What, No Orgy?', *National Review* 52.10 (2000), pp. 58–9, p. 59.

30 Rushton 2001, p. 35.

31 Elvis Mitchell, 'That Cruel Colosseum', *New York Times*, 5 May 2000.

32 Thomas Elsaesser, 'Specularity and Engulfment: Francis Ford Coppola and *Bram Stoker's Dracula*', in Neale and Smith 1998, pp. 191–208.

Chapter 6: *Fellini Satyricon*: 'Farewell to antiquity' or 'daily life in ancient Rome'?

1 Bordwell 2004.

2 See J.P. Sullivan, 'The Social Ambience of Petronius' *Satyricon* and *Fellini Satyricon*', in Martin Winkler (ed.), *Classical Myth and Culture in the Cinema* (Oxford, 2001), pp. 260–71, with a most useful bibliography. See also Wyke 1997, pp. 188–92; Joanna Paul, 'Rome Ruined and Fragmented: The Cinematic City in *Fellini's Satyricon* and *Roma*', in Richard Wrigley (ed.), *Cinematic Rome* (London, 2008), pp. 109–20.

3 Jon Solomon, *The Ancient World in the Cinema* (revised and expanded edition, New Haven, CT, 2001), p. 280

4 Most concisely, all three ideas can be found in the preface to the 'Treatment' published in Dario Zanelli (ed.), *Fellini's Satyricon* (New York, 1970).

5 See Paul 2008.

6   Pauline Kael, 'Fellini's Mondo Trasho', *New Yorker*, March 1970, p. 134.

7   Federico Fellini, *'Satyricon'*, *Playboy*, May 1970, pp. 105–11, p. 106.

8   For an overview of the history of moonlit visits to the Colosseum see Keith Hopkins and Mary Beard, *The Colosseum* (Harvard, 2005), pp. 1–20.

9   Fellini 1970, p. 106.

10 For instance: 'The ruins of the Colosseum? Picture postcards. Nothing was coming to me . . . save that vague sense of funereal melancholy that photographers have invented showing those ruins silhouetted at sunset with a couple of lambs in the foreground' (Fellini 1970, p. 106).

11 On Rome in Fellini's other films, see Elena Theodorakopoulos, 'The Sites and Sights of Rome in Fellini's Films', in David Larmour and Diana Spencer (eds), *The Sites of Rome: Time, Space, Memory* (Oxford, 2007), pp. 353–84.

12 The 1930 edition of Baedeker's *Guide to Rome and Central Italy* exhorts tourists to visit at night, when entrance is allowed, to retrace Byron's moonlit steps (no mention is made of Daisy Miller's unfortunate demise after just such a visit in Henry James' novella). By 1969 the Colosseum's official opening hours were restricted to daylight hours.

13 In Edmund White's autobiographical novel *The Farewell Symphony* (New York, 1997), the narrator recounts a nocturnal expedition through the city around midnight with the purpose of 'cruising'. He despairs over the discrepancy between the Rome of the movies and the decaying, grim reality of the place, and then describes his view across the flow of traffic to the moonlit Colosseum. Inside the structure he has a sexual encounter with a young man who pulls him 'between two columns into—what? The Emperor's box seat?' (White 1997, p. 98). I owe this reference to Elizabeth Speller.

14 From Fellini's letter introducing the project of *A Director's Notebook* to Peter Goldfarb, published (translated into French) in *Positif* 413–14 (July–August 1995), my translation.

15 Federico Fellini and Alberto Moravia, 'Documentary of a Dream', in Zanelli 1970, pp. 24–30.

16 Fellini and Moravia 1970 p. 26.

17 Ibid., pp. 28–9.

18 Ibid., p. 30.

19 Alberto Moravia, 'Dreaming up Petronius, in Peter Bondanella (ed.), *Federico Fellini: Essays in Criticism* (3rd edition, New York and London, 1978), pp. 161–8, p. 166. (the article was first published in *New York Review of Books*, 14.6 (26 March 1970), pp. 40–2).

20 See for instance Eileen Lanouette-Hughes, *On the Set of Fellini Satyricon* (New York, 1971), pp. 132 and 159.

21 Lanouette-Hughes 1971, p. 18.

22 Federico Fellini, 'Preface', in Zanelli 1970, p. 43.

23 Fellini and Moravia 1970, p. 26.

24 Fellini, 'Preface', in Zanelli 1970, p. 45.

25 Moravia 1978, p. 163. Wyke 1997 picks up on this formulation in the title of her final chapter.

26 See also Bernardino Zapponi's essay 'The Strange Journey', published in Zanelli 1970, pp. 33–9: 'No erudition, we had decided; no historical reconstruction . . .', p. 34.

27 There are many examples, for instance in Fellini 1970, p. 45; in Zanelli 1970, p. 8. See Wyke 1997 and Paul 2008 for more on this theme.

28 Moravia 1978, p. 164.

29 Federico Fellini and Bernardino Zapponi, 'Screenplay', in Zanelli 1970, p. 273.

30 Ibid.

31 Federico Fellini, 'Treatment', in Zanelli 1970, pp. 44–5.

32 Sullivan 2001. See also Jon Solomon, *The Ancient World in the Cinema* (New Haven, CT, 2001), pp. 276–9, for a good overview of the 'authentic' aspects of the film. See Lanouette-Hughes 1971, p. 32, where a collaborator is quoted as saying that 'much of Fellini's inspiration comes from Robert Graves' *Hadrian's Memoirs* and Jerome Carcopino's *Daily Life in Ancient Rome*. There's a million things he found in those books.' I imagine the source means Marguerite Yourcenar's *Memoirs of Hadrian*.

33 Published in English as Jerome Carcopino, *Daily Life in Ancient Rome: The People and the City at the Height of the Empire*, trans. E.O. Lorimer (London, 1991).

34 Carcopino 1991, p. 280.

35 Fellini in Zanelli 1970, p. 49, and Carcopino 1991, p. 263. It is perhaps unkind to point out that all the details that make their way into Fellini's (unrealised) scenario are to be found on the same page of Carcopino's book.

36 Fellini in Zanelli 1970, p. 48, and Carcopino 1991, p. 236.

37 Carcopino 1991, p. 254.

38 Ibid., p. 269, and Martial, *Epigrams* 1.21.

39 In the 'Treatment', Fellini envisages Mucius Scaevola burning his arm: 'In the last scene, the lead actor goes off stage and is replaced by a wretch whose arm is really burnt off, much to the delight of the audience' (Fellini in Zanelli 1970, p. 53).

40 Although Fellini claims that the suicides are Petronius himself and his wife.

41 Carcopino 1991, p. 101. See Pliny, *Letters*, 3.16 for his praise of Arria.

42 Gilles Deleuze, *Cinema II: The Time Image* (Minneapolis, 1989), p. 89.

Chapter 7: *Titus*: **Rome and the penny arcade**

1 John Wrathall, Review of *Titus* in *Sight and Sound* n.s. 10.10 (October 2000), p. 62.

2 See Robert Miola, *Shakespeare's Rome* (Cambridge, 1983), pp. 42–4, for an outline of the scholarly positions.

3 Wyke 1997, pp. 75–8.

4 Miola 1983, p. 75.

5 T.J.B. Spencer, 'Shakespeare and the Elizabethan Romans', *Shakespeare Survey* 10 (1957), pp. 27–38, p. 32.

6 Ibid.

7 Charles and Michelle Martindale, *Shakespeare and the Uses of Antiquity: An Introductory Essay* (London, 1990), p. 47.

8 See Miola 1983, p. 43.

9 See Martindale and Martindale 1990, pp. 121–5, on Shakespeare's uses of anachronism.

10 Ibid., p. 141.

11 David Fredrick, 'Titus Androgynous: Foul Mouths and Troubled Masculinity', *Arethusa* 41.1 (2008), pp. 205–33, p. 206.

12 See also ibid., pp. 213–15.

13 Ibid., p. 207.

14 Elsie Walker, '"Now is a Time to Storm": Julie Taymor's *Titus* (2000)', *Literature and Film Quarterly* 30.3 (2002), pp. 194–207, p. 194.

15 See Martindale and Martindale 1990, pp. 121–5.

16 Julie Taymor, *Titus: The Illustrated Screenplay, Adapted from the Play by William Shakespeare* (New York, 2000), p. 178.

17 Eileen Blumenthal and Julie Taymor, *Julie Taymor: Playing with Fire* (updated and expanded edition, New York, 1999), p. 144.

18 Jonathan Bate, 'Introduction', in Taymor 2000, p. 11. See also Solomon 2001, p. 281, who describes the costumes and sets of *Titus* as 'metahistorical'.

19 Sigmund Freud, *Civilisation and its Discontents* (1930); see Sigmund Freud, *Civilization and its Discontents*, trans. David McLintock (London, 2002), p. 8.

20 Taymor 2000, p. 178.

21 Ibid.

22 For an account of the theatrical production see Blumenthal and Taymor 1999, pp. 183–94.

23 Blumenthal and Taymor 1999, p. 220. See Walker 2002, pp. 197–8 on the 'staging' and 'framing' effects and the interplay between stylisation and realism.

24 For instance, David F. McCandless, 'A Tale of Two Tituses: Julie Taymor's Vision on Stage and Screen', *Shakespeare Quarterly* 53.4 (2002), pp. 487–511, p. 501, n. 26; Fredrick 2008, p. 224.

25 Walker 2002, p. 197.

26 Taymor 2000, p. 178.

27 Ibid., p. 179.

28 On the presence and absence of the audience in the arena see Judith Buchanan, *Shakespeare on Film* (London, 2005), pp. 247–8.

29 Walker 2002, p. 198.

30 Taymor 2000, p. 179.

31 Blumenthal and Taymor 1999, p. 186.

32 See McCandless 2002, pp. 495–6.

33 Taymor 2000, p. 185.

34 Ibid., p. 185: 'This time, the bleachers are filled with spectators. Watching. They are silent. They are we.' McCandless 2002, p. 500 is very interesting on the differences between the stage and the film version of this moment.

35 Fredrick 2008, p. 229.

36 Taymor 2000, p. 185.

37 McCandless 2002, p. 510.

38 Richard Burt, 'Shakespeare and the Holocaust: Julie Taymor's *Titus* is Beautiful or Shaksploi Meets (the) Camp', in Richard Burt (ed.), *Shakespeare After Mass Media* (London, 2002), pp. 295–329, p. 311.

Conclusion

1 Sobchack 1990, p. 24.

FURTHER READING AND VIEWING

Chapter 1: Narrative and spectacle, realism and illusion, and the historical film

For the politics and ideology of ancient Rome in film all students should read Maria Wyke's path-breaking book *Projecting the Past: Ancient Rome, Cinema and History* (1997). Issue 6 of the online journal *Screening the Past* is devoted to the debate about film and history and contains a number of key essays that give a good sense of what the issues are. I recommend Robert Rosenstone's book *History on Film/Film on History* (2006) as the most accessible and comprehensive treatment of the subject. On film style, David Bordwell's work is indispensable; his book, *The Way Hollywood Tells It* (2006) is a compelling and very informative read. On film narrative, Kristin Thompson's *Storytelling in the New Hollywood: Understanding Classical Narrative Technique* (1999) is equally valuable. For those who want to delve further into film theory there is a vast number of collections of key essays. I find Braudy and Cohen's *Film Theory and Criticism* (the most recent edition is 2004) a very useful tool. On the internet, there is a marvellous website called 'The American Widescreen Museum' (www.widescreenmuseum.com). It is full of fascinating and well-presented information on widescreen technologies. John Belton's book *Widescreen Cinema* (1992) will tell you everything you need to know about CinemaScope and the like.

Chapter 2: *Ben-Hur*: 'Tale of the Christ' or tale of Rome?

On biblical epics, Bruce Babington and Peter William Evans *Biblical Epics: Sacred Narrative in the Hollywood Cinema* (1993) is the key text. Willam Fitzgerald's excellent essay 'Oppositions, Anxieties, and Ambiguities in the Toga Movie' in the collection *Imperial Projections: Ancient Rome in Popular Culture*, edited by Joshel, Malamud, and McGuire (2001), is packed with interesting thoughts on *Ben-Hur*. Martin Winkler's 'The Roman Empire in American Cinema after 1945', which was republished in the same collection, is an essential text for all the films in this book. For those who want to know more about epic and masculinity, I recommend Leon Hunt's essay 'What are Big Boys Made of? *Spartacus*, *El Cid*, and the Male Epic' in the collection *You Tarzan: Masculinity, Movies, and Men,* edited by Pat Kirkham and Janet Thumin (1993). *The Robe* (1953) and *Quo Vadis* (1951) form a useful background. William Wyler's other Roman movie is *Roman Holiday* (1953), a very different experience of the city.

Chapter 3: *Spartacus* and the politics of story-telling

For anyone interested in learning more about *Spartacus*, Martin Winkler's *Spartacus: Film and History* (2007) collection is the best place to start. Alison Futrell's essay 'Seeing Red: Spartacus as Domestic Economist' in Joshel, Malamud and McGuire's *Imperial Projections* (2001) is essential. Ina Rae Hark's essay 'Animals or Romans: Looking at Masculinity in *Spartacus*', published in Cohan and Hark's *Screening the Male: Exploring Masculinities in Hollywood Cinema* (1993) explains the importance of the gaze in this film. Steve Neale's essay 'Masculinity as Spectacle' in the same collection provides an essential overview to this central topic. The Kubrick Site (http://www.visual-memory.co.uk/amk/) contains a wealth of material, including Duncan Cooper's essays on *Spartacus*, a number of interviews with Kubrick and some of his writing on film. The 2004 television version of *Spartacus* merits close viewing.

Chapter 4: *The Fall of the Roman Empire*: The filmmaker as historian

Martin Winkler is the main authority on *Fall of the Roman Empire*; his essay 'Cinema and the Fall of Rome', from *Transactions of the American Philological Society* (1995) to which I refer throughout is essential reading. Martin Winkler's collection *The Fall of the Roman Empire: Film and History* (2009) will undoubtedly become a key item on this film. On film and history, the items mentioned in the Further Reading and Viewing section for Chapter 1 are the most helpful. *El Cid* (1961) is usually considered Mann's more successful historical epic film. *Cleopatra* (1963) is roughly contemporary with *Fall* but is a very different sort of epic.

Chapter 5: *Gladiator*: Making it new?

Martin Winkler has collected some excellent essays in his volume *Gladiator*: *Film and History* (2004). In that volume Peter Rose's essay is especially worth reading as a critique of the politics of *Gladiator*. For those who want to know more about story-telling Jon Solomon's essay in the same volume on the development of the script is invaluable. David Bordwell's *The Way Hollywood Tells It* (2006) is the key text in understanding the style of *Gladiator*. I learned a great deal about contemporary film from two books especially: Steve Neale and Murray Smith's *Contemporary Hollywood Cinema* (1998) and Geoff King's *New Hollywood Cinema: An Introduction* (2002). Following up the endnotes to this chapter will lead the interested student to a range of other sources. The May 2000 issue of the journal *American Cinematographer* (81.5, 2000) contains a number of interesting articles on the production and design of *Gladiator* as well as an interview with the director. *Saving Private Ryan* (1998) was stylistically very influential for *Gladiator*. *The Patriot* (2000) and *Braveheart* (1995) are useful contexts, as is Ridley Scott's 2005 historical epic *Kingdom of Heaven*. The influence of *Gladiator* is visible in the production design of the television series *Rome* (2005–7).

Chapter 6: *Fellini Satyricon*: 'Farewell to antiquity' or 'daily life in ancient Rome'?

As an introduction to Italian cinema I recommend Peter Bondanella, *Italian Cinema* (3rd edition 2001). On Fellini there is a huge number of studies. The key items on *Satyricon* and *Roma* are published or republished in Bondanella's collection, *Federico Fellini. Essays in Criticism* (1978). Anyone interested in researching *Satyricon* further should start with J.P. Sullivan's important essay 'The Social Ambience of Petronius' *Satyricon* and *Fellini Satyricon*', published in Martin Winkler, *Classical Myth and Culture in the Cinema* (2001). *Satyricon* ought to be seen in context with Fellini's other films about Rome, especially *La Dolce Vita* (1960) and *Roma* (1972), but also *Nights of Cabiria* (1957). *Satyricon* influenced *Gladiator* and *Titus* and the grubbiness of its Roman streets can be found again in the *Rome* TV series (2005–7).

Chapter 7: *Titus*: Rome and the penny arcade

Jonathan Bate's edition of *Titus Andronicus* in the Arden Shakespeare series (1995) is an essential, rich and informative research tool. On Shakespeare and Rome, there are a number of excellent treatments. Robert Miola does fullest justice to *Titus Andronicus* in his book *Shakespeare's Rome* (1983) republished as a paperback in 2004. As an introduction to Shakespeare and the Romans, I also recommend Charles and Michelle Martindale's wonderful book *Shakespeare and the Uses of Antiquity: An Introductory Essay* (1990). A handful of essays on Taymor's *Titus* itself are mentioned in the notes; Elsie Walker's '"Now is a Time to Storm": Julie Taymor's *Titus* (2000)' (2002) is perhaps the most accessible of these. Taymor's own 2000 publication of the screenplay is gorgeously illustrated and the director's notes are illuminating. There are a number of interesting books on Shakespeare in film. Among those that mention *Titus* are Judith Buchanan's *Shakespeare on Film* (2005) and *New Wave Shakespeare on Screen*, by Thomas Cartelli and Katharine Rowe (2007). I think that *La Dolce Vita*, *Fellini Satyricon*, and *Roma* all play a part in *Titus*. David Fredrick demonstrates the significance of de Mille's *The Sign of the Cross* (1932) for *Titus*. Luciano Visconti's *The Damned* (1960) is often mentioned as an influence. Sir Laurence Olivier's *Henry V* (1944) is an important model for all modernised Shakespeare on film.

BIBLIOGRAPHY

Archer, Eugene, 'Hailed in Farewell: "Spartacus" Gets Praise of Pleased Director', *New York Times*, 2 October 1960.

Arnheim, Rudolf, *Film as Art* (Berkeley, 1957).

Babington, Bruce and Evans, Peter William, *Biblical Epics: Sacred Narrative in the Hollywood Cinema* (Manchester, 1993).

Bankston, Douglas, 'Death or Glory', *American Cinematographer* 81.5 (2000), pp. 34–45.

——'Veni, Vidi, Vici' [interview with Ridley Scott], *American Cinematographer* 81.5 (2000), pp. 46–53.

Barr, Charles, 'Cinemascope: Before and After', *Film Quarterly* 16.4 (summer 1963), pp. 4–24.

Barthes, Roland, *Roland Barthes by Roland Barthes*, trans. Richard Howard (Berkeley and Los Angeles, 1994).

Basinger, Jeanine, *Anthony Mann* (new expanded edition, Middletown, CT, 2007).

Bate, Jonathan, *Shakespeare and Ovid* (Oxford, 1993).

—— (ed.), *Titus Andronicus* (Arden Shakespeare edition, London, 1995).

——'Introduction', in Taymor 2000, pp. 8–13.

Bazin, André, 'Will CinemaScope Save the Film Industry?', trans. Bert Cardullo, *Film Philosophy* 6.2 (2002), at http://www.film-philosophy.com/vol6-2002/n2bazin (originally published as 'Cinémascope: sauvera-t-il le cinéma?', *Esprit* 21.207–8 (October–November 1953), pp. 672–83).

—— *What is Cinema?* Vols 1 and 2, trans. Hugh Gray (new edition, Berkeley and Los Angeles, 2004, first published 1967–71).

Belton, John, *Widescreen Cinema* (Cambridge, MA, 1992).

Blumenthal, Eileen and Taymor, Julie, *Julie Taymor: Playing with Fire* (updated and expanded edition, New York, 1999).

Bondandella, Peter (ed.), *Federico Fellini. Essays in Criticism* (3rd edition, Oxford and New York, 1978).

—— *The Eternal City: Roman Images in the Modern World* (Chapel Hill, NC, and London, 1987).

—— *The Cinema of Federico Fellini* (Princeton, 1992).

—— *Italian Cinema: From Neorealism to the Present* (3rd edition, London, 2001).

Bordwell, David, 'The Art Cinema as a Mode of Film Practice', in Braudy and Cohen 2004, pp. 774–82 (first published in *Film Criticism* 4.1 (1979), pp. 56–64).

—— *The Way Hollywood Tells it: Story and Style in Modern Movies* (Berkeley and Los Angeles, 2006).

——, Staiger, Janet and Thompson, Kristin, *The Classical Hollywood Cinema: Film Style and Mode of Production to 1960* (New York, 1985).

Braudy, Leo and Cohen, Marshall (eds), *Film Theory and Criticism: Introductory Readings* (New York and Oxford, 2004).

Buchanan, Judith, *Shakespeare on Film* (London, 2005).

Buckland, Warren, 'A Close Encounter with Raiders of the Lost Ark: Notes on Narrative Aspects of the New Hollywood Blockbuster', in Neale and Smith 1998, pp. 166–77.

Burt, Richard, 'Shakespeare and the Holocaust: Julie Taymor's *Titus* is Beautiful or Shakesploi Meets (the) Camp', in Richard Burt (ed.), *Shakespeare After Mass Media* (London, 2002), pp. 295–329.

Carcopino, Jerome, *Daily Life in Ancient Rome: The People and the City at the Height of the Empire*, trans. E.O. Lorimer (London, 1991).

Cartelli, Thomas and Rowe, Katharine, *New Wave Shakespeare on Screen* (Cambridge, 2007).

Cohan, Steven and Hark, Ina Rae (eds), *Screening the Male: Exploring Masculinities in Hollywood Cinema* (London, 1993).

Cooper, Duncan, 'Who Killed the Legend of Spartacus? Production, Censorship, and Reconstruction of Stanley Kubrick's Epic Film', in Winkler 2007, pp. 14–55.

Cyrino, Monica, '*Gladiator* and Contemporary American Society', in Winkler 2004, pp. 124–49.

Davis, Natalie Zenon, *Slaves on Screen* (Cambridge, MA, 2000).

Easthope, Anthony, 'Classic Film Theory and Semiotics', in Hill and Church Gibson 2000, pp. 49–55.

Edwards, Catharine (ed.), *Roman Presences: Receptions of Rome in European Culture, 1789–1945* (Cambridge, 1999).

Elley, Derek, *The Epic Film: Myth and History* (London, 1984).

Eldridge, David, *Hollywood's History Films* (London, 2006).

Elsaesser, Thomas 'Specularity and Engulfment: Francis Ford Coppola and *Bram Stoker's Dracula*', in Neale and Smith 1998, pp. 191–208.

Falsetto, Mario, *Stanley Kubrick: A Narrative and Stylistic Analysis* (new and expanded edition, Westport, CT, and London, 2001).

Fellini, Federico, '*Satyricon*', *Playboy* May 1970, pp. 105–11.

Felperin, Leslie, 'Decline and Brawl', *Sight and Sound*, n.s. 10.6 (2000), p. 34.

Fenwick, J.H. and Green-Armytage, J., 'Now You See It: Landscape and Anthony Mann', *Sight and Sound* 34.4 (1965), pp. 186–9.

Fitzgerald, William, 'Oppositions, Anxieties, and Ambiguities in the Toga Movie', in Joshel, Malamud and McGuire 2001, pp. 23–49.

Fredrick, David, 'Titus Androgynous: Foul Mouths and Troubled Masculinity', *Arethusa* 41.1 (2008), pp. 205–33.

Futrell, Alison, 'Seeing Red: Spartacus as Domestic Economist', in Joshel, Malamud and McGuire 2001, pp. 77–118.

Hark, Ina Rae, 'Animals or Romans: Looking at Masculinity in *Spartacus*', in Cohan and Hark 1993, pp. 151–72.

Herman, Jan, *A Talent for Trouble: Willam Wyler* (New York, 1997).

Hill, J. and Church Gibson, P. (eds), *Film Studies: Critical Approaches* (Oxford, 2000).

Hopkins, Keith and Beard, Mary, *The Colosseum* (New Haven, CT, 2005).

Hunt, Leon, 'What Are Big Boys Made of? *Spartacus*, *El Cid*, and the Male Epic', in Pat Kirkham and Janet Thumin (eds), *You Tarzan: Masculinity, Movies, and Men* (New York, 1993), pp. 65–83.

Joshel, Sandra, Malamud, Margaret and McGuire, Donald T. (eds), *Imperial Projections: Ancient Rome in Popular Culture* (Baltimore and London, 2001).

Keel, Anna and Strich, Christian (eds), *Fellini on Fellini*, trans. Isabel Quigley (London, 1976).

Kracauer, Siegfried, *Theory of Film: The Redemption of Physical Reality* (London, 1960).

King, Geoff, *New Hollywood Cinema: An Introduction* (New York, 2002).

Kubrick, Stanley, 'Notes on Film', *Observer Weekend Review*, 4 December 1960, p. 21.

—— 'Words and Movies', *Sight and Sound* 30.1 (1961), p. 14.

Landy, Marcia, *Italian Film* (Cambridge, 2000).

Lanouette-Hughes, Eileen, *On the Set of Fellini Satyricon* (New York, 1971).

Losemann, Volker, 'The Nazi Concept of Rome', in Edwards 1999, pp. 221–35.

McBride, Joseph, 'Fellini: *A Director's Notebook*', in Bondanella 1978.

McCandless, David F., 'A Tale of Two Tituses: Julie Taymor's Vision on Stage and Screen', *Shakespeare Quarterly* 53.4 (2002), pp. 487–511.

MacCabe, Colin 'Realism and the Cinema: Notes on some Brechtian Theses', *Screen* 15.2 (1974), pp. 7–27.

Magid, Ron, 'Rebuilding Ancient Rome', *American Cinematographer* 81.5 (2000), pp. 54–9.

Marcus, Millicent, *Italian Film in the Light of Neorealism* (Princeton, 1986).

Martindale, Charles and Martindale, Michelle, *Shakespeare and the Uses of Antiquity: An Introductory Essay* (London, 1990).

Mast, Gerald, 'Kracauer's Two Tendencies and the Early History of Film Narrative', *Critical Inquiry* 6.3 (1980), pp. 455–76.

Miola, Robert, *Shakespeare's Rome* (Cambridge, 1983).

Mitchell, Elvis, 'That Cruel Colosseum' [review of *Gladiator*], *New York Times*, 5 May 2000.

Moravia, Alberto 'Dreaming up Petronius, in Bondanella 1978, pp. 161–8 (first published in *New York Review of Books* 14.6 (26 March 1970), pp. 40–2).

Mulvey, Laura, 'Visual Pleasure and Narrative Cinema', *Screen* 16.3 (1975), pp. 6–18.

Muschamp, H., 'The Epic: Throwing Our Anxieties to the Lions', *New York Times*, 30 April 2000.

Neale, Steve, *Genre* (Chippenham, 1980).

—— 'Masculinity as Spectacle', in Cohan and Hark 1993, pp. 9–22.

—— *Genre and Hollywood* (London and New York, 2000).

Neale, Steve and Smith, Murray, *Contemporary Hollywood Cinema* (London, 1998).

Nelson, Thomas Allen, *Kubrick: Inside a Film Artist's Maze* (Bloomington, IN, 1982).

Paul, Joanna, 'Rome Ruined and Fragmented: the Cinematic City in *Fellini's Satyricon* and *Roma*', in Richard Wrigley (ed.), *Cinematic Rome* (London, 2008), pp. 109–20.

Pomeroy, Arthur J., 'The Vision of a Fascist Rome in *Gladiator*', in Winkler 2004, pp. 111–23.

Pierson, M., 'A Production Designer's Cinema: Historical Authenticity in Popular Films Set in the Past', in Geoffrey King (ed.), *Spectacle of the Real: From Hollywood to Reality TV and Beyond* (Bristol, 2005), pp. 145–55.

Rose, Peter W., 'The Politics of *Gladiator*', in Winkler 2004, pp. 150–72.

Rosen, Philip, *Change Mummified: Cinema, Historicity, Theory* (Minneapolis and London, 2001).

Rosenstone, Robert, 'History in Images/History in Words', *American Historial Review* 93.5 (1988), pp. 1173–185.

—— *History on Film/Film on History* (Harlow, 2006).

Rosenthal, Stuart, 'Spectacle: Magnifying the Personal Vision', in Bondanella 1978, pp. 289–302.

Rushton, Richard, 'Narrative and Spectacle in *Gladiator*', *CineAction* 56 (2001), pp. 35–43.

Sadashige, Jacqui, 'Review of *Gladiator*', *American Historical Review* 105.4 (2000), pp. 1437–8.

Sheehan, Henry, 'Roman Games', *Sight and Sound*, n.s. 1.4 (1991), pp. 22–5.

Simon, John, 'What, No Orgy?', *National Review*, 52.10 (2000), pp. 58–9.

Sobchack, Vivian, '"Surge and Splendor": A Phenomenology of the Hollywood Historical Epic', *Representations* 29 (1990), pp. 24–49.

—— 'The Insistent Fringe: Moving Images and the Palimpsest of Historical Consciousness', *Screening the Past* 6 (1999), at http://www.latrobe.edu.au/screeningthepast/.

Solomon, Jon, *The Ancient World in the Cinema* (Yale, 2001).

—— '*Gladiator* from Screenplay to Screen', in Winkler 2004, pp. 1–15.

Sorlin, Pierre, *The Film in History: Restaging the Past* (Oxford, 1980).

Spencer, T.J.B., 'Shakespeare and the Elizabethan Romans', *Shakespeare Survey* 10 (1957), pp. 27–38.

Staiger, Janet, 'Securing the Fictional Narrative as a Tale of the Historical Real', *South Atlantic Quarterly* 88.2 (1989), pp. 393–413.

Stone, Marla, 'A Flexible Rome: Fascism and the Cult of Romanità', in Edwards 1999, pp. 205–20.

Strick, Philip and Houston, Penelope, 'Interview with Stanley Kubrick Regarding *A Clockwork Orange*', *Sight and Sound* 41.2 (1972), pp. 62–6.

Sullivan, J.P., 'The Social Ambience of Petronius' *Satyricon* and *Fellini Satyricon*', in Winkler 2001, pp. 260–71.

Taymor, Julie, *Titus: The Illustrated Screenplay, Adapted from the Play by William Shakespeare* (New York, 2000).

Theodorakopoulos, Elena, 'The Sites and Sights of Rome in Fellini's Films', in David Larmour and Diana Spencer (eds), *The Sites of Rome: Time, Space, Memory* (Oxford, 2007), pp. 353–84.

Thompson, Kristin, *Storytelling in the New Hollywood: Understanding Classical Narrative Technique* (Cambridge, MA, 1999).

Thomson, David 'The Riddler Has his Day', *Sight and Sound* n.s. 11.4 (April 2001), pp. 18–21.

Walker, Elsie '"Now is a Time to Storm": Julie Taymor's *Titus* (2000)', *Literature and Film Quarterly* 30.3 (2002), pp. 194–207.

White, Edmund, *The Farewell Symphony* (New York, 1997).

White, Hayden, *The Content of the Form* (Baltimore, 1987).

—— *Metahistory: The Historical Imagination in Nineteenth Century Europe* (Baltimore, 1975).

Willeman, Paul, 'Anthony Mann—Looking at the Male', *Framework* 15–17 (summer 1981), pp. 16–20.

Winkler, Martin, 'Mythic and Cinematic Traditions in Anthony Mann's *El Cid*', *Mosaic* 26.3 (1993), pp. 89–111.

—— 'Cinema and the Fall of Rome', *Transactions of the American Philological Society* 125 (1995), pp. 135–54.

—— 'The Roman Empire in American Cinema after 1945', *Classical Journal* 93.2 (1997), pp. 167–96.

—— (ed.), *Classical Myth and Culture in the Cinema* (Oxford and New York, 2001) (a revised edition of *Classics and Cinema* (Lewisburg, 1991).

—— *Gladiator: Film and History* (Oxford, 2004).

—— *Spartacus: Film and History* (Oxford, 2007).

—— *The Fall of the Roman Empire: Film and History* (Oxford 2009).

Wood, Michael, *America in the Movies: Or, 'Santa Maria, It Had Slipped my Mind'* (London, 1975).

Wrathall, John, 'Bloody Arcades' [interview with Julie Taymor], *Sight and Sound* n.s. 10.7 (July 2000), pp. 24–6.

—— 'Review of *Titus*', *Sight and Sound*, n.s. 10.10 (October 2000), p. 62.

Wyke, Maria, *Projecting the Past: Ancient Rome, Cinema and History* (London, 1997).

—— 'Ancient Rome and the Traditions of Film History', *Screening the Past* 6 (1999), at http://www.latrobe.edu.au/screeningthepast/.

—— 'Are You Not Entertained?: Classicists and Cinema', *International Journal of the Classical Tradition* 9.3 (2003), pp. 430–45.

—— 'Film Style and Fascism: *Julius Caesar* (1953)', *Film Studies* 4 (2004), pp. 58–74.

Zanelli, Dario (ed.), *Fellini's Satyricon* (New York, 1970).

FILMOGRAPHY

This filmography lists the main films discussed in the book.

Ben-Hur (1959) dir. William Wyler, produced by Sam Zimbalist, MGM.

Cleopatra (1963) dir. Joseph L. Mankiewicz, produced by Walter Wanger, 20th Century Fox.

La Dolce Vita (1960) dir. Federico Fellini, produced by Guiseppe Amato, Franco Magli, Angelo Rizzoli for Riama Film, Pathé Consortium Cinéma, Gray-Film.

The Fall of the Roman Empire (1964) dir. Anthony Mann, produced by Samuel Bronston, Samuel Bronston Productions.

Fellini: A Director's Notebook (Block-notes di un regista) (1969), dir. Federico Fellini, produced by Peter Goldfarb, NBC.

Fellini Satyricon (1969) dir. Federico Fellini, produced by Alberto Grimaldi, Les Productions Artistes Associés.

Gladiator (2000) dir. Ridley Scott, produced by Walter Parkes, DreamWorks SKG.

The Patriot (2000) dir. Robert Emmerich, Columbia Pictures Corporation.

Quo Vadis (1951) dir. Mervyn LeRoy, produced by Sam Zimbalist, MGM.

The Robe (1953) dir. Henry Koster, produced by Frank Ross, 20th Century Fox.

Roma (1972) dir. Federico Fellini, produced by Turi Vasile, Francese.

Rome (2005–7), TV series, produced by Bruno Heller, BBC/HBO.

Saving Private Ryan (1998) dir. Steven Spielberg, produced by Steven Spielberg, Amblin Entertainment/DreamWorks SKG.

Spartacus (1960) dir. Stanley Kubrick, produced by Kirk Douglas, Bryna Productions.

Spartacus (2004), TV drama, dir. Robert Dornhelm, USA Network Pictures.

Titanic (1997) dir. James Cameron, produced by James Cameron and John Landau, 20th Century Fox.

Titus (1999) dir. Julie Taymor, produced by Julie Taymor, Clear Blue Sky Productions.

INDEX